SKIP THE PAIN, EXPERIENCE THE PLEASURE

Cut the Crap that's
Holding You Back
so You Can Live the
Life You Love

Christa

First published by Ultimate World Publishing 2023
Copyright © 2023 Christa Roseborsky

ISBN

Paperback: 978-1-923123-09-0
Ebook: 978-1-923123-10-6

Christa Roseborsky has asserted her rights under the Copyright, Designs and Patents Act 1988 to be identified as the author of this work. The information in this book is based on the author's experiences and opinions. The publisher specifically disclaims responsibility for any adverse consequences which may result from use of the information contained herein. Permission to use information has been sought by the author. Any breaches will be rectified in further editions of the book.

All rights reserved. No part of this publication may be reproduced, stored in or introduced into a retrieval system, or transmitted in any form, or by any means (electronic, mechanical, photocopying, recording or otherwise) without the prior written permission of the author. Any person who does any unauthorized act in relation to this publication may be liable to criminal prosecution and civil claims for damages. Enquiries should be made through the publisher.

Cover design: Ultimate World Publishing
Layout and typesetting: Ultimate World Publishing
Editor: Rebecca Low

Ultimate World Publishing
Diamond Creek,
Victoria Australia 3089
www.writeabook.com.au

TESTIMONIALS

"This book is meant for every walk of life! One that will give you aha moments that will impact your life, long after you close the book."

Stuart Graham – Ontario, Canada

I normally have difficulty reading more than 10 pages, but this book carried the core of me to its end in just one sitting. As I flipped the final page, I yearned for more. The yearning was more than just to read her stories filled with that wit and wisdom... but deep down to continue embracing a precious 4-year-old, who felt abandoned in that moment she picked glasses off her driveway, to unconditionally love her throughout each dark night of the soul.

G. Williams – Ontario, Canada

Skip The Pain, Experience The Pleasure

"I was spellbound and struck by how many difficulties the author weathered in her life. Her experiences made it real, and this book touched me in a profound way. Going forward, I'll see adversity with a new set of lenses and be better equipped to roll with whatever life throws my way."

Laurie Ann Mclean – Mexico

"Engaging, inspiring, and hilarious can sum this book up. It was such a quick easy to read book, that can benefit anyone! I have been fortunate not to have had the struggles Christa writes about, but how she outlined how to have the best life grabbed me and now I'm following this advice. "

Maike Dombrowsky – Canada

"Inspiring and captivating! I'm awestruck at how the author traversed such incredible challenges and captured these life lessons with such humor."

Silvia Valdman – Switzerland

"Wow! Such a much-needed bright light of inspiration for this world!"

Sylvia Parker – Ontario, Canada"

"While reading Christa's story, my heart was breaking for her, but then she found a way to infuse strength and humor into her story. She teaches the reader how to not only cope but survive and thrive despite chronic pain and illness. Christa

Testimonials

has an uncanny ability to find grace and humor even in the most dire circumstances. Her strength is like no one I have ever known. The funny stories, acronyms, and strategies she shares are unique and valuable. This book can help people to shift their perspective and find grace, humor, hope, and comfort when coping with traumatic life events."

Julie Diaz, Author and Certified Health Coach – New Jersey

"Wow! What a captivating read—I couldn't put the book down. So much wisdom captured in this one book has reshaped my own perspective on my life. Practising gratitude is my key takeaway which I will leverage to open the door to new possibilities for me."

Otgonbaatar Norjinjav – Mongolia

"In a blunt way, she showed me that pain is pain. We can live life either by focusing on it which holds us back or using the lessons to create the life we want!"

Elliott Clarke – Ontario, Canada

"The author's wit makes for such an attractive read! I love the puns and innuendos, especially in the chapter titles. What's riveting, is how the author transforms life's tragedies into triumphs using perspective – being mindful of that inner voice, avoid dwelling on the negative and being grateful will shape how happy you'll be."

A. & M. Plzak – Mexico

DEDICATION

To my family, friends, and everyone who crossed my path, who supported me in my journey to heal so I can inspire others facing any sort of pain to find hope by sharing some of the things I've learned.
To my readers who identify with the feelings, laugh through the pain and find courage to share their take-aways long after reading this book.
To myself for being vulnerable.

DISCLAIMER

Some of the names, descriptions and details may have been changed to protect the identities of others.

CONTENTS

Testimonials	iii
Dedication	vii
Disclaimer	ix
Introduction	1
Chapter 1: 10 Seconds of Pleasure or Pain	5
Chapter 2: Wax Job	17
Chapter 3: Blow Off Your Job	33
Chapter 4: The G Spot	45
Chapter 5: Stop Licking My Wounds	55
Chapter 6: Vitality and Vigor	65
Chapter 7: Give Up Hope	77
Chapter 8: Wait For It!	89
Chapter 9: Pleasing Myself	117
Chapter 10: F@!&%^! Is Your Answer	135
Chapter 11: Climax of Life	145
Chapter 12: Don't Let Others Hold the Pen	159
Conclusion	171
More Testimonials	175
About the Author	179
Speaker Bio	181

INTRODUCTION

Have you ever had that feeling that life has pulled the rug out from under you? And while you're busy wondering how hard you're going to land; some invisible force has already executed its plan to roll you up like some poorly twisted burrito on Taco Tuesday with the bonus of "Our Extra Spicy Hot Sauce" that's hot going in and hot going out! You know that feeling?

Well, I've been there, that's why I wrote **Skip the Pain, Experience the Pleasure**: *Cut the Crap that's Holding You Back so You Can Live the Life You Love!* I know, add it to the pile of "New Age Woo-Woo Literature", am I right??

But this is something different; a totally new paradigm of thinking...*Skip the Pain, Experience the Pleasure* is perfect for you. Why the heck did I write this book? Well over and over,

Skip The Pain, Experience The Pleasure

people told me to and I was even approached by a publisher and figured ok. I did it and it sucked.

I mean it made me depressed and I didn't need any help. I stopped and was told, "Your story might be someone else's road map." I'm sure they read some quotes, but it got me thinking, when I went through my stuff, there were a lot of books telling the story of the traumas, but nothing that was blunt, to the point, or anything I could identify with! So, if I could help one person, even if it was me writing this, I needed to do it.

My gut wouldn't let it go, so here it is, warts and all!! It's quick, easy to read, and full of life-changing insight. I will share with you the tools needed to overcome all obstacles and provide you with step-by-step methods to inspire the way you live, discover your purpose, achieve your goals, and sharpen your awareness to create your best life!

You'll naturally notice that the way you speak will change. Not taking things so personally and asking for what you need are the pillars of peace and freedom. The key is to explore your unique values. Once you see how your emotions and feelings impact your thoughts, beliefs, and actions, you'll be motivated to step into your power, change those pesky habits and achieve your dreams.

You'll finally be able to smash the mask that hides your insecurities that yes, we all have. The more you actually use these skills—not just let them hide in some pages, the more you'll feel like a rock star with confidence. You'll have no doubt in your mind that your identity is not wrapped up in your job, role in the family, or diagnosis.

Introduction

An accident or global pandemic will remind you of what's most important to you in life. I'm sure you'll easily relate and have those quick skills at your fingertips to pass on after reading *Skip the Pain, Experience the Pleasure. Cut the crap that's holding you back so you can live the life you love!*

Chapter 1

10 SECONDS OF PLEASURE OR PAIN

Less than 10 Seconds can change your life.
How do you deal with it?

If you want to know the value of one year, just ask a student who failed a course.
If you want to know the value of one month, ask a mother who gave birth to a premature baby.
If you want to know the value of an hour, ask the student waiting to find out if they were accepted to their dream school.
If you want to know the value of one-hundredth of a second, ask the athlete who placed second place in the 100 meters in the Olympics.
If you want to know the value of eternity, just ask me about writing this book!

Slippery Spring

I clearly remember leaving the hospital I worked at around 7 pm. It was well after hearing of this massive snowstorm that hit a few hours before. Ironically, it was the first day of spring. I kept thinking we should be seeing budding flowers, not searching for snow blowers!

Before I walked out, I yelled, "Please be careful driving home!" to the rest of the staff. My socks got soaking wet as I trudged through the slick, white fluff. I mean, who wears boots on the first day of spring? Not me obviously. The roads didn't look that bad. Most were clear until I left the city and started driving on the county road where I lived. There were mostly fields, and it was beautiful to see the snow drifting, looking like rippling waves; it was so serene.

My mind was already planning dinner or what leftovers we had. I think I had put some chicken in a Crockpot that day, a working mom's saving grace for providing a home-cooked meal. These seemed like the most important things as I felt my wheels slip a bit under my car. It was enough to shake me out of my wandering mind, forcing me to focus on the road. It was only then that I noticed that my car was skating on a sheet of ice, and as I tried to gain control, I felt the spin and then a sudden halt as a snowdrift stopped my descent into the ditch. My heart was pounding. I pushed on the gas, but nothing.

I'll never forget the lights, the bright headlights that seemed to be larger than life. Were they coming towards me? Omg, yes, they were. I reached to jump out of the car, but my instincts stopped me. I held both hands on the steering wheel, planted my feet on the floor, closed my eyes, and thought, this is it.

The truck hit me head-on. My small car looked like a crushed can. I had to be taken out of the back door because there was no opening left in the front. A passing car stopped and called 911, and the ambulance took me back to the hospital I had just left.

This ordinary first day of spring turned into the last day I labeled myself as being "there". This car accident was so much more than getting hit head-on by a pickup truck. It was me getting hit head-on by life. All my pain I kept stuffing down, my fears I ran from, my skeletons I bolted in closets, and my insecurities that were hidden by my mask.

I wore a heavy weight on my back, the label of a wife, mother, and professional, and set the bar quite high for myself to be the "perfect" everything, to make up for the imperfect truth. My whole life turned around. I learned how important it is to not take for granted what I used to think of as the small things in life. It's so easy to go through the day complaining, whining, and feeling resentful until you're faced with a crushing immense reality.

Coping with Pain

So, how did I cope with the pain from my car accident?

Spinach, kale, seaweed, and beets. Why couldn't I have become addicted to any of these? My body and mind craved anything to stop the pain. I could barely lift my head; the whiplash felt like a vice around my neck. The trauma to my bruised body triggered flare-ups from my Lyme disease and then they told me I had something called fibromyalgia. I was used to fighting pain from Lyme, but with everything stacked together, it was as if I was on the floor after losing a boxing match with a grizzly bear.

I started doing anything I could to numb the pain, so I went to my doctor, and he prescribed pain medicine.

I stayed busy so I didn't have a second to think. Later, I broke down in exhaustion as my emotions started to claw their way up to the surface. I opened a bottle of wine because, of course, it's never a good idea to keep things bottled up, right? Oh boy, that routine didn't end well.

I started spiraling down. The lights, the sound, and the smell of the burning tires seemed so real. I started having flashbacks from childhood issues, abuse, and things that didn't even seem to be related to the accident. Memories I stuffed down seemed to haunt me. I had a hard time bending over to bathe our son. My drug of choice was validation with worry mixed in. "I'm fine," was my favorite line but in my mind, I was shouting, "for the love of God, I'm going insane!"

I was worried about what others thought of me, it was like I had an "Approval-O-Meter". I cranked the handle with every dish I cleaned or even when I would do my best to make dinner, only to forget the instructions on how to make it outlined on the back of the box that I already threw out and yes, sometimes I had to pluck it back out of the trash. (I can't be the only one, right?) just so someone would acknowledge how great I was healing, and that I was the wonderful wife and mother I so desperately wanted to be.

The pride I had felt for always being the strong one completely collapsed, so I broke down and went to see a counsellor. I remember walking in nervously, wanting to take something to calm down but figured that wasn't a good idea. She was sweet, in her 40s, and she made me feel comfortable. About 20 minutes into the conversation, I started opening up, not just about the car accident but about a whole bunch of things that I went through in life. It was relieving. She abruptly stopped me and asked if I would mind if she took a quick break because if she didn't take one now, the smokers in her building would, and she would miss her chance. She handed me some books and told me what chapters to read until she got back. I smiled as she left, but I was confused. I mean, I was scheduled for an hour. I stared at the pale-yellow chipped paint on the walls and wondered if I just wasn't worth the whole hour. I wasn't worth the smoker break, I wasn't worth her time, I wasn't worth it.

As she came in, I quickly wiped my eyes as she apologized. "Are you ok?" she asked. "Yeah, I was having pain from my whiplash, I'm fine."

I wasn't lying about the whiplash part but for me, **FINE** stood for **F**reaked out, **I**nsecure, **N**eurotic, and **E**motional, but I didn't want to make her feel bad. I really wanted some sort of validation that I at least asked for help but didn't get it. She grabbed me an ice pack and it was just enough to focus on the cold drips that fell around my neck to keep my emotions in check. I asked, "So am I fixed?"

She smirked and said, "Absolutely not, come back weekly so we can explore all your issues, oh and don't forget to check it out with your insurance for coverage." Then the session was finally over. I told her I didn't have my calendar so I would call for the next appointment. I never did.

I went back to my doctor to tell him the pain pills weren't working, and I saw his right eyebrow lift and his lips purse shut. He told me to wait there, which usually meant running like hell, but I waited. He came in with a neatly stapled pile of papers that said Recovery. "Recovery from what, my car accident?" I blurted out.

He said, "Yes, actually the addiction to the pills, and anything you're doing to stop the pain."

No way. It wasn't like I was on street drugs (whatever that meant), and it wasn't like I was draining our account from gambling or had a shopping addiction. I was in real pain!

I was in complete denial. "I just don't want to feel!" I said with a cracked voice, trying not to cry.

Ding Ding! I got it as it slipped out of my lips. I felt as if he was telling me that I failed. I realized, of course, that what I was doing wasn't working, so with my husband's push, I agreed to try another way. It turned out that it was about me finding healthy ways to cope with feelings and emotional pain, not just physical pain. Even when I tried to shake it off, nothing and no amount of running away from my body or mind helped. Not even spinach. Screw you, Popeye!

DENIAL: **D**on't **E**ven **K**now **I A**m **L**ying

I was in complete denial. I wasn't looking for the feeling of being high, or even happy. I was searching for the feeling of numbness, getting my mind to stop, to just be and escape.

For me, DENIAL stands for **D**on't **E**ven **K**now **I A**m **L**ying. I really felt I had it all together and that lasted all about 45 seconds, the best 45 seconds of my life! I went to a recovery home and there were people there just like me who had been through tragic events, horrible abuse, and addictions of all sorts. It didn't matter what happened. Pain is pain, suffering is suffering, trauma is trauma but what differs is how it affects you. I wasn't aware when I was in **denial**, sometimes the truth hurts. I thanked God that I got help because I had no idea there was a lot more to come.

Why do I share this? It's because I was terrified to ask for help for fear of being judged.

I could have left this out of this book, but for those who stuff things behind locked doors, I want you to know that it's ok to unlock those fears and shame to get help. It stopped my spiral and prevented things from getting even worse. It didn't mean I was weak. It meant I was strong.

Take the Scenic Route

I thought back to a time after college. A group of us were going to Myrtle Beach just before graduation. With no GPS, we relied on our map, which was folded at least 50 times with highlighted routes all over it. From where I live, it should have taken us approximately 13 hours, but it took us 20!

Skip The Pain, Experience The Pleasure

Yes, we got lost. Many, many, many times. I swear some of the most beautiful paths we found wouldn't have been discovered without getting lost. We stopped in a little town to get gas and said to a guy, "We can't find this road on the map!"

He said, "Well little ladies, that's because it's not on the map!"

That's how far off we were. The people we saw on open roads, or one-lane gravel roads surrounded by a canopy of trees were like a trip itself! We laughed, cried, bared our souls, solved the world's problems, created our own problems, filled our faces with gas station junk food, and did car karaoke.

On the way home, we thought we were tanned, but no, we were burnt! Life lesson: don't fall asleep on the beach! We slathered ourselves with aloe vera to stop some of the skin from peeling off but then my friend's legs swelled up bigger than a blowfish on steroids! She was allergic to aloe, and this was not the best time to find out.

So, I had to drive. Did I mention it was a stick shift and I barely knew the basics? I mean these were some crazy highways we were going through. You could hear the screech of the transmission as I attempted to pay at one of the tolls. Then crap, I stalled it again, and the familiar song of honking and colorful words came back. Sometimes she would shift, and I would press the clutch. Then when we had to go uphill, I prayed to every god, universe, sun, higher power, and angels of the roads that I

10 Seconds of Pleasure or Pain

wouldn't roll backward! In the end, the best part of our trip wasn't where we planned to go but all the wild stuff (we'll keep most of that between us) that happened along the way.

I'm type A, meaning I like having everything planned out, but in this case, no matter how much highlighting I did, the Gods of the roads had a different plan. You see, it's like how my life seemed to go. I thought I would end up where I wanted to go, but as it turns out, with a few wrong turns, I ended up much wiser and where I *needed to* be. And looking back, it's beautiful.

I was thinking back to that crazy adventure and wondered where those days went. Usually "spontaneous" and "Christa" were never used in the same sentence.

It was a normal Friday night, and my husband Rob grabbed a beer and chips and then chillaxed in his green leather recliner. It had been about five years since we went anywhere, which was our honeymoon. Out of nowhere, I blurted out, "If you could go on a vacation anywhere right now, where would you go? I definitely caught him off guard.

He said, "Well, I always wanted to go to British Columbia. Why? Where would you want to go?"

> "I believe life is better when you turn up the music, eat too much chocolate, walk barefoot, talk about weird sh!t with weird people, hug strangers, and go on adventures. Those things won't make life perfect, but they sure as hell make this ride more fun!"
> — BROOKE HAMPTON

My mind flew back to when I was in grade eight and we were asked the same question and said, "The West Edmonton Mall".

Skip The Pain, Experience The Pleasure

It was the largest mall in the world at that time, and I loved to shop! It also had a skating arena and a water park. It seemed like a utopia to me. I don't know what came over me, but I said, "Let's do it!" I wasn't even fully recovered from my accident.

"What, right now? Yeah, I'll believe you mean it when pigs fly," Rob said sarcastically.

I meant it, so we cracked open that piggy bank, stuffed our bags, packed our son, and off we went to the airport.

"This is the bomb!" our son belted out. If there was a sign, this was one of the words under the category of *what not to say in an airport*!

We got on the plane and instead of stuffing our faces with gas station food, we upgraded to airport food and finally, we were off on our dream vacation.

It might not have been a big deal for some people, but it was perfect for us. We had so many laughs at Rob going up and down the waterslide and having so much fun. Even though I was still using a cane, I didn't let that stop me from going around that mall and the whole trip was exactly like I pictured it, except I was with my family. We returned home and things were different, things were lighter. Looking back now, I realize I had gained a new perspective. I saw that it was the best decision because I would have regretted not making those memories.

Summary of Insights

- **The most cherished value is time. It can change without a moment's notice. It's easy to spend 10 seconds complaining or harboring resentment but that's 10 seconds of time you lost.**

- **It can be any type of crash in life that can bring up unresolved pain. It's ok to ask for help instead of trying to numb it. Even if you're in denial, it doesn't mean you're weak, it means you're strong.**

- **Sometimes the route you think you're on can change, and you can end up in the most beautiful place. Enjoy the journey, not just the destination.**

- **Go for it! Be intentional and spontaneous with those you love. It could be a trip to the backyard or around the world. The place doesn't matter. Memories are more important than materials.**

Chapter 2

WAX JOB

Sometimes, letting go is painful but ends up being smooth and beautiful.

I had to start learning to let go. I loved Lori, my hairdresser. Over the years, I think I became her therapist as she would share her latest boy drama, roommate drama, and how she can't even bake a cake from a box. I shared some of my drama, and in the end, somewhere, I got my haircut. She would cut it, layer it, defuse it and it would end up looking like a fuzzy Q-tip on my head. I would pay, give her a tip with a small smile, and drive home to wash it.

I tried styling it the way I wanted but with those short layers, it was no use. The next time, I brought in a picture of a girl who had the hairstyle I wanted. The therapy session went on, and when I looked in the mirror, my Q-tip hair was back. I held up the picture to compare and she said, "Yes I did it perfectly, actually better because I gave it volume," and she emphasized the word *volume*!

Again, I was left frustrated. Lori was a sweetheart, but my hair was far from sweet! I saw an old friend who had the style of hair I loved, and she quickly gave me the number of her hairstylist. Now, what do I do? I felt like a hair whore! But yes, I threw my hair in a messy bun and canceled my next appointment with Lori. I let her down easily, saying I was helping a friend who just opened a business. It was the best move I made! No more Q-tip head for me!

Surround Yourself with Good People

I had to break up with friends too, or they eventually broke up with me. Sound weird? Sound familiar? There were those sleepovers where I wrote in a friend's journal, BFF (best friends forever). Well, as we grew up, forever only lasted a few years. Some of my true friendships are based on a solid foundation of alcohol, sarcasm, and inappropriate shenanigans. There were times I didn't see it, but people were just using me. I'm not here to blame others. It made me feel good, and it made me feel wanted and needed. I held them in my life for too long. I would feel drained, like being with a vampire who sucked the soul out of me, and there were times it clouded my actions.

Their part in the story of my life may be over but my story goes on. On the other hand, I'm fortunate that I have some lifetime friends that are always there, even if we might not see each other a lot. We all have the next chapters in our lives, and for whatever reason, some people slip through the cracks. As you go through your journey, surround yourself with good people. People who lift you up, tell you when you have spinach stuck between your front teeth, help you grow, and allow you to be your authentic self. I found my tribe.

> "One day, all of us will get separated from each other. We will miss our conversations. Days, months, and years will pass until we rarely see each other. One day, our children will see our photos and ask, "Who are these people?" And we will smile with invisible tears and say, "It was with them that I had the best days of my life."
>
> UNKNOWN

I Signed Up to Be a Wife and Mother - Not a Widow and Single Parent!

It's hard not to question why when things seem to fall apart. Sometimes I can get superstitious. I find myself wondering if all of this wouldn't be happening if I had only forwarded that chain email to 10 people. Heck, they warned me! Everyone has their dream, usually, something they never had. Some people want a monkey, some a Porsche, or maybe they want a monkey chauffeur driving a Porsche! Whatever peels your banana!

Skip The Pain, Experience The Pleasure

As for me, I never experienced the ideal family, with a mom and dad sitting at the table listening to their children's day. I wanted that more than ever. I finally got it as an adult. I was married to my love, we had a son, and we were renovating our dream home. When I say "home" that word is something I always wanted to experience. Growing up, there weren't many homes with divorced parents, and without getting into my childhood drama, let me just say it was *anything* like living in a home. You would think I would have appreciated life just a bit more after my car accident, but sometimes it's easier to drive down the highway while only using the rear-view mirror to navigate.

It was one year, one month, and one day after my car accident when I got that call. Two weeks prior, Rob seemed tired and overall sick, which was weird because he would normally go non-stop. I dragged him to the doctor after it seemed to linger. At first, she said just to rest, but after a few days, I noticed he was losing his appetite. He became weaker and had a slightly yellowish color. Dr. Google gave me the diagnosis, he definitely had mono! He went for a blood test, and they immediately told him to go to the hospital. They admitted him and did many other tests, including a bone marrow biopsy. The doctor called us both in and said this was the saddest news he had ever given to a young couple.

Rob had a fast and aggressive form of leukemia and he had already had it for three or four months. The doctor said there wasn't much time, but they were still going to try chemotherapy and all other available treatments. We needed one more day at home, and reluctantly, the doctor gave him the last transfusion before we left. We had to keep our emotions in check as we were rushing against the clock for my husband to show me files, passwords, and so many other things that I needed to know. Those 24 hours flew by so fast, but not because we were having fun. Then he gave me the best gift of all. We talked and he told me even though he was going to fight this, if he doesn't make it, he wanted me to get remarried. I told him never and he will get better! I didn't want to think of the possibility of losing him. His voice softened and he told me to move to the city, get a condo, or stay at our farm. This is the true definition of unconditional love. He looked at me and asked, "What if you died in your car accident? Wouldn't you want me to remarry?"

I jokingly said, "As long as she wasn't bigger than a C cup!"

Two weeks after his diagnosis, I was called by the doctor at the hospital, which was ironically the same one I worked at, and was brought back to after my car accident. I called my in-laws as he started to lose consciousness, and I stood by his side when he started having seizures. The doctors ordered a CAT scan to see if there was any bleeding in his brain. We were waiting for the elevator to go back up, and I held his hand and put my head close to his. I always told him to fight, but this time I whispered, "It's ok, you gave me a beautiful son and showed me what true love is. If it's time, you can go."

We shared an intimate moment as he crossed from this life to the next. For a split second, I felt intense love. I was certain I was able to feel his transition into this other realm of pure love and light. I didn't want to face reality, but I had to. The hardest thing I had to do was tell our son that Daddy went to heaven. Both our hearts were crushed as I held him in my arms.

Does it matter what kind of loss sparks the emotion of grief? No. It could be having a miscarriage, losing a parent, a friend, or a pet, going through a divorce, or experiencing any crushing disappointment. Heck, my best friend lost all the pictures she had stored when her computer crashed and that was devastating! Ok, maybe not quite the same but you get it. What matters is how it affects you.

WAX JOB - GOOD GRIEF

A few months later, I decided to get a hamster, something for both my son and I to care for, until unfortunately, his life was cut short. We drove up to the drive-through window of Canada's favorite local coffee and doughnut shop as we reached for our 10-pack of donut holes. I slowly passed them to the backseat where our glossy-eyed son sat. As he opened the box and grabbed a doughnut, there was a slight smile as he picked his favorite one, but our smiles quickly faded as I knew he was eating out of a coffin. Waffles, our beloved hamster died, I'm sure in a peaceful way, but his little heart was broken.

"Are we going to have a funeral?" My son asked.

I was a bit shocked and said, "Well of course," even though secretly, I wondered…how is this going to work out?

There we were, slowly putting the hamster in the tiny donut box, as I dug out a hole. We gathered around and reminisced about funny memories of how Waffles would crawl all over him, and how he hung on top bars of his cage, trying to go from bar to bar like a gymnast.

As we covered the box with dirt, we headed back to the house, and right away, he started asking if we could please get another hamster. All I could think of was we were finally free of the mess of the wood chips and stinky poop.

"I don't think it's a good idea right now," I said without even making eye contact.

"Please!" he begged and started getting angry at the fact that I was apparently being an unreasonable parent.

Yes, I felt guilty, but as soon as the newest gadget came out, his focus changed. He now accepted that Waffles was gone, but still reminded me of it every time we drove by a pet store. From that day on, we didn't dare buy a 10-pack of donut holes!

You can look up any information about grief and you'll find the stages of grief. They are denial, anger, bargaining, depression, and acceptance. As you saw from the grieving of our hamster Waffles, our son went through his own stages of grief. From my experience, it wasn't always in this order, and sometimes, I bounced back and forth. I know it on an intellectual level but knowing it and experiencing it are totally different.

It's like going for a wax job. You know it's going to be painful but until you've had those hairs ripped off your skin and then try to ease the pain with some cream, lotion, lube, or whatever, you just don't get it. Once you experience it, it's so much more than learning about it.

Looking back, the memories made during our Edmonton trip changed my life. Not just the fun parts, but the action of fulfilling our dreams. Even though I still had to be the responsible one, I never forgot to take the time to do what filled my heart. We honored our intuition and took our last family trip in January. Rob died in April. We were left with no regrets.

So, How Did I Cope with Losing My Husband?

I started my journey of self-help. I started looking at what hospice had to offer. I received invitations to classes from friends and caring people. I did exactly what I was told. I started by writing every affirmation on my mirror and high-fived myself. I read notes from loved ones, wrote notes to loved ones, and wrote notes to those I hated. Maybe I didn't hate all of them, but I was releasing anger. I took the papers and burned them. I wrote poems and shoved them in balloons and watched them float away, even though I knew they would get caught up in some tree. I held hands and sang Kumbaya songs that healed the soul. I cried, or at least tried to, because everyone else was, and sometimes my tears were just stuck. I went on retreats where I married myself and expressed my feelings in creative ways, like placing stones on a beach that said SOS! I hugged my inner child, and I hugged a tree.

I talked about feelings, then I was told they weren't feelings, and I was handed a list of feelings. I felt like shit. That wasn't on the list but that's what I felt! Being an overachiever, I memorized that list and prepared for what feelings I was going to have when it was my turn.

I woke up, gave myself a high five in the mirror, chanting my lipstick mirror affirmations with all the perfect sayings, and kept going. I kept going so fast that I fell apart, and I mean, there wasn't a feeling I could even put a name to. I just smeared the lipstick messages and ripped up those letters. There's no cookie-cutter approach to grief. Then I found a group for young widows and widowers, and finally, I didn't feel so alone.

I also knew there were no rules about feelings. Sometimes sad, sometimes pissed off at God, the doctors, and me. On the first garbage day, I was extremely angry that Rob wasn't there to bring the garbage down our long driveway. Then I felt guilty, I mean what a stupid little thing! Yes, that stupid little thing represented so much more. I ended up going back to work at the same hospital that I was brought to after my car accident, after which I spiraled down, and then lost my husband there. It was like a full circle. Normally I would have avoided that, but I went forward. I had to overcome the fear of judgment. Fortunately, people were compassionate, and I quickly went back to my normal work routine.

Be Vulnerable

Let yourself feel, get angry, and do what you need to do. What I didn't realize was having fun was being vulnerable too! I took my son to a water park. I couldn't fill my bathing suit top, and my white body was blinding. I hid under the towel, when I heard, "Please come in," and after about the 20th time, I gave in. I went down the big slides and laughed all the way down. Then I remembered how Rob took him down the slide only months ago. Tears filled my eyes, and my laughter turned into silence. Deep down I felt guilty for having fun, I mean it was only a few months! My son came up and looked me right in the eyes and said, "I want to have fun like Daddy did but now you get to!" From then on, I allowed myself to feel whatever it was, even happiness in the midst of grieving.

Never Say Never

I learned you can never fix a broken heart. I thought I would never get married again. I had no idea what my next move would be, and I took it very seriously because it would also affect my son. There I was, hoping the universe would step in and guide me as life continued.

I shifted areas of work, and I ended up meeting an amazing man who accepted my son and me. He didn't use those stupid pick-up lines; unlike the time I had my driveway done. The guy "accidentally" left his measuring tape at my house. He came back to pick it up and figured he might as well do the same to me as he said casually since he was done with the job, we should have dinner. "Oops big mistake," I whispered under my breath, as he glanced down at his hand which was holding the elusive measuring tape, both of us realizing he forgot to take off his wedding ring! Bye-Bye. There were a lot of creeps along the way before I met Darrin.

I felt like damaged goods. I mean I came with baggage and trauma...not the kind of relationship you would want to jump into. I guess the universe had its own idea. I had a friend who was going through a messy divorce, and I basically believed all men were scum, when she asked if I wanted to go for a drink. We went to a small pub, one with a parking lot (not like Downtown) and as soon as we sat down, of course, some greasy-haired guys sauntered over, so we got up and moved to a table near a friend she recognized.

"Can we sit with you, so we don't get bugged by guys? We're kind of on a man-hating night." They laughed and as the night went on, so did we.

One guy, Darrin, was particularly nice, and by the end of the night, he said, "You were great to hang out with, can I have your number?"

"Fine you probably won't call anyways," I said as I still had a chip on my shoulder about men.

Well, that chip cracked and seven years later, I married my best friend and was blessed with two more children. That's where I started to live the life I love, but we'll get to that later. Even though it was scary, it goes to show you to never say never!

Give Someone the Benefit of the Doubt

It was the anniversary of my first husband's death. I bought my son a helium balloon so we could attach a message and let it float up to heaven while visiting his grave (even though I wondered if it would end up tangled in some tree, but it made my son feel better). I pulled into a parking spot, only to hear a huge, long honk behind me!

"That was my spot you selfish b*tch!"

Then this man got out of his car, followed me, and continued to scream about how I cut him off and it was his parking spot. I apologized as I didn't even notice him. Then I teared up, not because I was upset about the parking spot, it was the one string that plucked at my heart as I was trying to be strong for my son.

I walked into the store, and in front of my son, he said, "Watch it, lady, you shouldn't be so selfish!" as he grabbed the cart I was going to take. He didn't realize he was crushing my soul. Not only was I still struggling with the grieving process, but I also now felt like a terrible human being. Yes, I might have taken it too personally, because realistically, it was only a parking spot, but geez!

So, this guy saw this woman who was probably a bitch taking his parking spot. He had no idea what I was really going through. He only saw things from his own perspective. My immediate reaction was, *seriously, he didn't have to act like a jerk*, but I quickly reframed it. I said to myself, that poor guy, he must be having a horrible day. Maybe he's at a dead-end job, marriage, or going through something crappy to lead to him acting like that. I felt better, and that might have been true! Even if it wasn't the case, I was able to let it go, instead of stewing over how much of a jerk he was. But the "poor guy" attitude changed it all around. So next time someone cuts you off or takes your place in line, say to yourself, poor guy, he/she must be going through something horrible to be acting like that. I guarantee empathy feels better than anger.

Don't you hate it when there's that one driver who speeds past you, weaves in and out of cars, and seems to have no care for anyone else but themselves? Can you imagine giving those reckless people the benefit of the doubt? Well, I have a confession. My husband was one of those people with me cheering him on!

You see, it was May 14 at 6 AM when I swore, I was going to give birth to my daughter right there in the car! When he stopped at a red light, I begged him to just go! There wasn't a person to be seen, and he saw the fear and pain on my face, so he hit the gas. I have a heart condition that needs to be monitored in the hospital. So, I want to apologize to everybody on that date for being the one who sped past you, maybe even weaved in front of you too quickly to get off at our exit. And to all those police officers, I don't condone running a red light. At the end of the day, we had a very healthy baby girl after mama arrived safely at the hospital.

Would You Rather Have Peace or Be Right?

I have learned in life that it is better to be the observer and give yourself time to formulate responses, and sometimes the right thing to do is not to respond at all, inner peace comes with knowing the difference. Well, it definitely was an interesting barbeque! There was this one guy who seemed like he was a walking encyclopedia of fad diets and magic weight-loss pills, slipping in that he was selling them. He kept talking about the latest trends and recommended anything, including some weird diet involving only eating blueberries on odd-numbered days. It was all I could do to keep a straight face. When I left, my friend asked me, "You know more about nutrition than anyone else here, why didn't you say anything?"

I simply shrugged and replied, "Well, I was there to enjoy the food and company, not to win a nutrition debate, even though I will admit it was like dinner and a comedy show! After all, sometimes it's far more important to have peace than to be the almighty right. Plus, who knows, maybe one day blueberry-only odd-days diets will be the next big thing!"

We both burst into laughter, realizing the absurdity of it all. When I left, I took the lesson I learned. It's better to find peace than to be right, even if I snickered on the inside. I also had to put my sunglasses on to hide when I was tempted to roll my eyes! In the end, we all had a good time, with blueberries or not.

Summary of Insights

- **Remember people come into your life for a reason, season, or lifetime. Surround yourself with those who inspire your greatness, accept you without judgement and let go of those people who become a burden and hold you back.**

- **The stages of grief are like a wax job. You never know the true pain until you've experienced the hurt ripped off you. But know it too shall pass and will ultimately make you more resilient.**

- **Never say never! Sometimes the universe has extraordinary plans for you just waiting around the corner.**

- **Be patient! Give people the benefit of the doubt. You have no idea what someone is going through, and one day it might be you.**

- **It's more important to have peace than to be right. In the long run, you will live with less chaos and more serenity.**

Chapter 3

BLOW OFF YOUR JOB

Your name badge isn't your identity.

Half the time when I meet someone, they ask what I do for a living and barely ask for my name. Yes, it's a social norm, but think about the stay-at-home parents, or people that are on disability, in between jobs, or going back to school. Does it matter? Is that how you judge them? Many of us do. It's crazy but so many people define themselves by what they do, like a label on their head, "Hi I'm a dog groomer, I'm a doctor, I'm some important person that I hope you ask what I do." It was embarrassing when I bumped into one of the gentlemen and couldn't remember his name but felt like saying, "Hi gynecologist". It was fine because I got a, "Hey you, nice to see yah," fully knowing he didn't remember my name either.

Skip The Pain, Experience The Pleasure

Even before we finish school, we make career choices based on deeply embedded beliefs that come from our friends (what will they think?), parents (what do they expect from me?), and community (is this considered a "real" job?). Then we spend so much time and money just to have an office plastered with framed degrees, diplomas, certificates, etc. Then what? Do any of these papers prepare us for the real world? Do they challenge us to look hard at what our passion is and what natural gifts we have? We hear all sorts of messages that make us feel as if our choices are limited and we "should" devote our lives to whatever work is expected.

> "Here's to the crazy ones, the misfits, the rebels, the troublemakers, and the round peg in square holes...the ones who see things differently. They're not fond of the rules. You can quote them, disagree with them, glorify, or vilify them, but the only thing you cannot do is ignore them because they change things. They push the human race forward, and while some may see them as the crazy ones, we see genius."
> — STEVE JOBS

Many secretly wish they could change directions, but because they connect their identity with their title, they push down their dreams. They may eventually fall off that wheel and burn out. Or some universal twist in life that's completely unexpected could cause a breakdown.

This breakdown can cause a breakthrough! You don't have to wait for some accident or tragedy to wake up and decide to examine your life and make the changes you always wanted to. If you need permission, then I'll give it to you. Trust me; it's better to make a plan to change or venture into a new career when you're able, instead of dreaming about it from a hospital bed.

Imposter Syndrome! Check! Got it!

> "To make money we lose our health, and then to restore health we lose our money. We live as if we're never going to die and die as if we never lived."
> — UNKNOWN

Sounds like this could belong in the trailer for a mystery movie. I walked into work, hobbling like a wobbly toddler when I looked down and noticed I had two different shoes on, one brown and one black. And to add insult to injury, they were two different heels! I made it through trying to conceal my miscalculated shoes. I was the last to leave work, now having toe cramps from scrunching them under my desk when I had this weird thought, *maybe I'm really not as good as I think I am. Actually, what if I'm not as good as everyone else thinks I am? What if they find out the truth that I really don't know what I'm doing? I mean, I can barely put on the right shoes!* Yes, my mind will spin all the way down that rabbit hole, thinking that I'm a fake!

Self-doubt engulfed me as I compared myself to other successful colleagues. The next day, after one of our meetings, one of the directors pulled me aside and said, "I didn't understand one thing in that meeting!" I blurted out my insecurities, and we both laughed because in my mind, she had it all together, and she saw me as the one who could make anything successful. There's actually a name for it. It's called Imposter Syndrome.

By some formal definition, it's that deep feeling of being inadequate or not belonging, hiding just beneath the surface.

As I researched it, I realized it's normal to feel this way. Whew, I was not alone. The best part was I became more open with others when they had doubts and saw their Eureka moment!

Ironically, I always felt that I had to do more in any job. Looking back, I've successfully managed hundreds of people throughout my career.

Also, I've opened three different buildings with a team including departments for hospitals, long-term care , and becoming the Director Of Nutrition as well as opened a restaurant. I can't even begin to count the number of people I interviewed, created job descriptions, and how many projects I was responsible for. I became a Certified Coach Practitioner as well as a Leadership Coach. My only thought was to succeed, not only for me but for everything I was part of. This is not to brag, but to put highlights for me because I was stuck in believing my job was my identity. My work ethic is ingrained in me no matter what I'm doing but it doesn't have anything to do with what name badge I have. Eventually, I discovered my true gifts of intuition and became an energy worker in many modalities, as well as studied herbalism but we'll get into that later.

In every job, there are parts of what we do that we hate. It's those parts that we should focus on doing our best job! I've learned to give a hundred percent, well unless I'm giving blood. Without even realizing it, you're doing something valuable that's part of a chain for the greater good. So, if you do it half-assed, it's like biting into an apple only to find half a worm. Don't believe me, just read this newspaper article then ask yourself if you want to be the one to check every thermometer and work in quality control.

> **When you have an 'I hate my job' day ...**
>
> Try this out:
> Stop at your pharmacy, go to the thermometer section and purchase a rectal thermometer made by Johnson & Johnson.
>
> Be very sure you get this brand.
>
> When you get home, lock your doors, draw the curtains and disconnect the phone so you will not be disturbed.
>
> Change into comfortable clothing and sit in your favorite chair. Open the package and remove the thermometer. Then, carefully place it on a table or a surface so that it will not become chipped or broken.
>
> Now the fun part begins.
>
> Take out the literature from the box and read it carefully. You will notice that in small print there is a statement:
>
> "Every rectal thermometer made by Johnson & Johnson is personally tested and then sanitized."
>
> Now, close your eyes and repeat out loud five times, "I am so glad I do not work in the thermometer quality control department at Johnson & Johnson."

Article Unknown Author

From Hero to Zero

An old friend's son Zack was a football player who didn't make the cut and lost his scholarship. It's not always a job that can shift the way you identify yourself, it could be anything, even a sport. He went from superstar to the one who almost made it. After years of practicing, traveling, attending summer camps, and a whole hell of a lot of money spent, Zack sat in his coach's office and balled like a child. You see, football

Skip The Pain, Experience The Pleasure

wasn't just a sport; he wasn't just part of a team. It became his family. This was a lesson that life can change directions, whether you plan for it or not.

> "Work for a cause, not applause. Live life to express, not to impress. Don't strive to make your presence noticed, just make your absence felt."
>
> Unknown

So, insert any life change. I'm not talking about hormonally; you know what I mean. Realistically, at some point, whatever you've devoted yourself to will be over. Kids will grow up and move out, you might retire, get laid off, get fired, go on disability, or graduate, it doesn't matter what you did. I know it sucks, it's hard to think that there's life after whatever you've devoted so much of your time to. Maybe you're throwing a party celebrating the end of some job you went into day in and day out. It could've been soul-sucking, or soul-fulfilling. But now you're questioning, who the heck am I now? I'm here to tell you that you're still the same person; you're just doing something different within the next 24 hours. You still might be an astrophysicist who loves gardening, so wake up and prune your bush!

This could be a way that the universe is telling you, "Hey you, follow me, and let's have some fun!" You know those dreams you thought you would never be able to do? It doesn't matter if it's a hobby, volunteering, going back to school, traveling, golfing, or starting a new business selling puppies.

Maybe you're thinking, but I still need to make money! If you worry about being poor, maybe look at it like **POOR - Passing Over Opportunities Readily**. So, there you go, check out those possibilities. And when nothing goes right, go left!

No qualifications are needed! Dreaming about starting a business but don't feel educated enough? Education is great, but so is desire. Don't discount experience and passion. Look at Thomas Edison who invented the light bulb and more. He only went to school for three months. We would still be in the dark without him! Life experience counts too. Change your age! Just because you're older doesn't mean you have less of a chance to be successful, it simply means you've had more time to learn a few lessons along the way. Look at Ray Kroc. He created the now-famous fast-food chain McDonald's when he was 52.

Take a chance! If you avoid failure, you'll also avoid success! Sure, it's scary, and you may lack confidence, but confidence is simply a willingness to be uncomfortable. Let that sink in. Change is right on the edge of your comfort zone.

> "When I was 5 years old, my mother always told me that happiness was the key to life. When I went to school, they would ask me what I wanted to do when I grew up. I wrote down "happy". They told me I didn't understand the assignment, and I told them they didn't understand life."
>
> JOHN LENNON

Ask, Don't Make Assumptions

This was a biggie for me. Yah, we've all heard "just ask" but often, it isn't that easy. The smallest chance of looking dumb, weak, or even rejected holds so many people back. Beating around the bush was easier for me and that didn't work. Now, finding the courage after all those thoughts racing around my brain was another thing. My biggest hurdle to get over was feeling like I was bothering someone or that others needed it more. From asking how to use the hole puncher to what button to press to make the space shuttle take off, we all need some help. The universe always wants to provide you with the solution, but don't be afraid to ask!

Do You See the Whole Truth or Assume the Worst?

> "We tend to make assumptions about everything. The problem with making assumptions is that we believe they are the truth. We could swear they are real. We make assumptions about what others are doing or thinking — we take it personally — then we blame them and react by sending emotional poison with our words. That's why whenever we make assumptions, we're asking for problems. We make an assumption, we misunderstand, we take it personally, and we end up creating a whole big drama for nothing."
>
> Don Miguel Ruiz

It seemed like a no-brainer for me what medicine to give someone when they were sick. When I was first dating my second husband, he was nice enough to come over and help me and my son because I had the flu. I *assumed* he knew what medicine to give me. In between hurling, I asked him to give me medicine for my stomach, like the brand, Gravol, we use from the top shelf, in the box of the hall closet. I couldn't open my eyes because my head was pounding so much. I felt a large pill come close to my lips and asked, "What is this?"

Blow Off Your Job

He said it was Gravol. Ok, maybe I was too sick to tell. He gave it to me, and I quickly spit it out as the pill was huge! "This can't be Gravol! It's normally a small pill!"

He went and got the box. He pointed out that it said Gravol, but what he didn't notice was it said suppositories. Yup, the wrong end! I just assumed he knew what pill it was. I married him anyway! (I'm not going to assume you know what a suppository is, just look it up, and it will make more sense.)

Sometimes we have biases about things which can change our beliefs. I love Mexican food, and I'm lucky enough to have some girlfriends who were just as excited to get out and have some flaming cheese with me! There was this one restaurant, nothing fancy but it had the best food. About a month earlier on the news, we heard of a shooting right in the same area as the restaurant. We picked a date and went but took every precaution. We had our plan to drive on well-lit roads and safer highways. I mean this was flaming cheese we were talking about! As we got off our exit, we realized quickly it was the wrong one. For the love of God, you have to be kidding; of course, the one road we landed on was the one where the shooting happened. We took a deep breath and cautiously drove.

At a stop sign, we were looking for directions when we heard a bang, bang, bang, we were sure we were getting shot at, so we all ducked down in the car. My heart was beating so fast I thought it was going to explode. We stopped and looked up. Nobody was around but we could still hear the banging, though it was starting to fade away. It took about two seconds for my friend to remember that when we were deciding which way to go, she pointed to the right, and hit her wooden beaded

Skip The Pain, Experience The Pleasure

rosary that was hanging in her rear-view mirror. That was it! It was the beads hitting the window, not shots! With a deep breath, we started to laugh. We made it to the restaurant safely but kept laughing. We went into the area assuming it was dangerous but if we had never seen it on the news, shots wouldn't have even entered our minds!

Summary of Insights

- Your identity is not linked to your name badge or job.

- Imposter syndrome? Welcome to the human race. At times we all don't feel confident in what we're doing.

- Change what you do in your 24 hours. It's just another opportunity to explore something different.

- Asking for help will save you a lot of time and guesswork. Even superheroes need help!

- It's easy to have pre-conceived opinions about people, places, and things but all we're doing is assuming that it is fact. This can change our outlook, experience, and reality.

Chapter 4

THE G SPOT

Gratitude is the highest form of happiness.

"Be grateful for the problems you didn't have."

Bug Guts

We drove home from one of my appointments, and the next day, I looked at my windshield and there were splattered bugs stuck on it; I mean it looked like a bug cemetery. The more I tried to use my wipers, the more they smeared. Great, I thought, as I went back into the house, achy and tired from the car ride home. When I looked outside, it was raining, I mean pouring. The downpour was only about 10 minutes before the sun started peeking out. I went back to my car and

Skip The Pain, Experience The Pleasure

the windshield was clean! I was never so grateful for rain for washing my bug guts so I could see and didn't have to deal with them myself. Who would have thought such a little thing would be something I was actually grateful for?

It's sometimes hard to find things we're grateful for in everyday life because the world is so full of things we wish we could have instead of the gifts we already have, even a clean windshield. The most important lesson that changed my life entirely is to be grateful. Period. It doesn't matter if it's that parking spot someone let you have, the dime you found, the blanket you wrapped yourself up with while waiting at the food bank, or the name-brand coat you wrapped yourself up with while waiting for your table at the restaurant. Maybe the heart transplant will save the life of the one you love. Even the hero that killed the giant spider that was going to eat you alive! Thank them! No, not just the little things, anything, and everything.

Now, are you keeping all that gratitude to yourself? Give it away freely.

"I wanted to let you know I've been thinking about you. I really appreciate everything you've done for me, and I don't know if I've ever told you that." This was a message I left for someone that popped into my head but made the conscious decision to let them know.

Think about what you have and be grateful for it. There's always someone who has it worse off than you. Right now, you might be living paycheck to

> "Feeling gratitude and not expressing it's like wrapping a present and not giving it."
> WILLIAM ARTHUR WARD

The G Spot

paycheck, barely being able to afford your home, utilities, internet, phone, and all that comes with it but there's someone who would love to be living like that. They can't even put a roof over their head, and your life would be their dream.

The insight that turned me on the most is that when I'm grateful, I find happiness, and being in a state of happiness and love is the greatest pleasure I can feel.

"I'm just having a good hair day," or, "This old thing?" are things I used to say if someone complimented my hair or clothes. Why was I making an excuse? I notice when others do that, I feel as if my compliment wasn't received. Once I realized this, I started to simply say, "Thank you!" instead of making up an excuse. Sure, it felt uncomfortable at first, but I didn't want to rob the other person of the experience of giving gratitude!

> One of my favorite life lessons that I've learned is just for a moment, imagine if you lost everything you have right now, and then got it back again. How grateful would you be? For me, that says it all.

After an exhausting plane trip, I experienced reality shock! I was fortunate to go on a mission to Costa Rica where we stopped off at one of the schools. This building had no doors or windows, and the dry heat poured in from the cut-out openings with material covering them that would never shield them from the weather. In one classroom, there was quite a mixed bag! There were tiny tots and big kids, kindergarteners and highschoolers, all crammed in there together like sardines in a can.

We all brought paper, crayons, pencils, sharpeners, and amongst other things, bouncy balls! I loved watching their eyes light up when I showed them pictures of snow, especially snowmen, and tobogganing. When we went out to eat, water was more expensive than pop! And what did we crave? Yes, water. I became so conscious of how much water we waste when we came home that I would yell from four rooms away to shut the water off!

We went to an open field and planted some trees. One of my missions is to plant 100,000 trees around the world, so we have some in Costa Rica! At the end of the day, it reminded us of how grateful we should be for what we have, even for something as simple as drinking water.

You're alive. You can get this book. No matter how challenging your life may feel, see your life clearly. Focus on the many things you have to be grateful for!

Fear and Fearless

I can think of countless ways fear has held me back in my life. Want to read my mind? Here are my fear-based beliefs, which now, looking back, made me miss many opportunities.

I wouldn't try out for something if I thought there was a chance I would fail.

- What if they rejected me?
- What if I fail?
- What would they think of me?
- How would they judge me?

- Who can I really trust?
- FOMO – Fear of missing out!

FEAR stands for **F**alse **E**vidence **A**ppearing **R**eal! Think about it, if you're scared of spiders, it's when you don't see them anymore that makes them scarier! So, when you do see it, face it, or at least keep an eye on it while screaming, "Spider!" like it's a fire.

Take risks to honor your true desires because no one said on their deathbed, "Yeah! I made it through life without a scratch!"

Put that damn swimsuit on like you know you want to do, and cannonball into the water. Just ask yourself, is this bringing joy to my life? Get messy, smudge that makeup, and don't wait for a pedicure. Walk in the grass. Get up early for some time just for yourself. Join in on the zip line instead of watching from the sidelines.

Everything you ever wanted is just on the other side of fear.

Facing my Fear

Ok, here's my epic adventure that shoved fear right in my face. It was at the beautiful Grand Canyon, and just like the brochures, it promised a once-in-a-lifetime experience. That experience was sitting right in front of me, a small eight-seater plane that promised to show me this wonder of the world in an up close and personal way. It was my birthday, and my husband said, "I surprised you with something you'll never forget."

Skip The Pain, Experience The Pleasure

He was right. A private plane ride to discover the Grand Canyon.

"Um thanks," I said as my mind was thinking of any excuse not to climb into my coffin.

You see, I was nervous, to begin with flying, but this tinier-than-a-dinky plane made it seem like a nightmare. But what could I do? I mean he went through all this effort, and I'm sure money.

So, there I was, walking around the plane, looking for any loose screws, scratches, or dings—maybe from birds. Then I met the pilot. I almost asked him for ID, he looked like I could be his mother!

"Looking forward to it, this will be my first tour!" he boasted.

That was it, the world was spinning. "Just kidding, get in, and for the birthday girl, she gets to sit next to me to have the full experience."

I literally threw up a little, looking back at my smiling husband anticipating this epic ride.

"Maybe tomorrow, I have a headache." (I could only use that excuse so many times.)

"You'll be fine, what's the worst that can happen?" The child-like pilot said as he climbed in.

My husband sprang in the back waiting for the take-off. We placed headphones on, and Mr. Pilot said, "On your mark, get set, and then the jerking of the plane started.

The G Spot

"You didn't say go!" I braced myself as my heart was literally beating out of my chest.

Music started to play. First, it was Sarah McLachlan, *In the Arms of an Angel,* followed by a more upbeat song, Nickelback, *If Today Was Your Last Day.* The fear of plunging into the Grand Canyon overcame me, but I tried to rationalize it by thinking this would be a great headline, "Plane swan dives in the Grand Canyon on Christa's birthday, a wish she wasn't expecting."

Ok, back to the rational mind. I did manage to pry open my eyes and yes, it was beautiful. I saw some breathtaking red and brown hills. As we completed the tour, heading back to safety, the pilot put his hands on his head and said, "Now you take the controls!"

WHAT???? Could someone please hand me a diaper? Fear didn't even cut it, insanity maybe. I shook as I grabbed the controls. I saw the fear in the six other people's eyes. He gave me the Coles Notes version as the plane tipped from side to side just enough for him to remind passengers there was a paper bag in front of them in case they needed to hurl. Where was my bag?

He saw a mountain and said, "You better get to whatever height because we don't want to crash into it." So, like a video game (which I always lost at), I pulled just as he instructed. My hands were sweaty, my heart was racing, and I shook all over but for a split second, the excitement came over me. I was flying a plane! Yes, I knew he could take over at any time, but that didn't seem to register. I didn't even notice the music turn upbeat. It was AC/DC's *Highway to Hell.*

Skip The Pain, Experience The Pleasure

He relieved me from my duties, and I relieved myself a little. We hit the runway with adrenaline pumping through my veins. I could barely breathe as I stepped out like a drunken sailor trying to get my sea legs. OMG, I did it, I thought with tears drizzling down my face. I didn't know if I wanted to hug my husband or throttle him when he said he had this whole thing set up.

So, when I thought, I was going to die and the bogus stories I was telling myself were fear, and that fear would have held me back, I knew the regret of not going through with the experience would be forever. At the end of the day, I felt fearless, proud, and glorious for facing my fear, not killing my husband, or anyone else for that matter, and stepping on that plane even though every part of my body and soul said not to because I was too scared. I can look back and proudly say I did it instead of I wish I did that when I saw those brochures stacked up.

Summary of Insights

- **Being grateful for what you have is the best way to achieve peace and happiness.**

- **What you have is someone else's dream.**

- **Facing your fears can prove there's nothing you can't get through.**

- **Once you do, you can see that the fear was just False Evidence Appearing Real.**

- **The feeling of excitement and accomplishment always outweighs fear and regret from stopping you.**

Chapter 5

STOP LICKING MY WOUNDS

Accepting and letting go of past stories.

Make peace with your past so it doesn't screw up your future.

Hangxiety: the stress of hanging onto shit that's not in alignment with our highest self.

Everything I went through is part of my story. It's my choice if I want to keep those stories alive or close that chapter. Seriously, why am I wasting time holding on to that one stupid, embarrassing story that happened like a zillion years ago?

Skip The Pain, Experience The Pleasure

When I was born, I only had 10% hearing in one ear, and it affected my speech. I had surgery and took speech lessons up until eighth grade, then quit after some girl saw me leave with a kindergarten book I used to help pronounce letters. Of course, she had to tease me about reading. As if that wasn't bad enough for a 13-year-old, I was chosen to read a speech in the church at our Confirmation. I overcame most speech impediments, but I still had trouble with ch, sh, r's and a few other letters.

Well, during the reading, it was supposed to say *then the church, it*...But as I nervously read, I blended it, and it came out, *"The shit!"* Lord help me! I froze, and the priest corrected me, and I finished the reading quickly like a robot, and sat down with tears coming down my face. Really, out of all the words I could have screwed up during a mass it had to come out that way!

Yup, to this day, I still shiver when I hear anything close to those letters and will avoid them at all costs, even if I have to say that "thingy". Stupid, right? I mean children are starving across the world and I'm having nightmares about this! At times I still replay the past, but it seems to focus on the "bad parts" rather than my joyful experiences. And seriously, did most people actually listen to the reading? If so, I'm sure they're not thinking about it now, they have their own embarrassing stories.

Forever Feeling

"I'm leaving," I heard my mom say as she went out the door. When I was young, there weren't many kids who had divorced parents. I ran downstairs and saw her sunglasses in the driveway. I chased her a bit before my dad called me to go back inside. I went into my room and sat on my light green Berber rug. That's it? Will I see her again? I didn't even get to say goodbye!

As I wiped my tears, all I could think of was what was going to happen to me and my brother. Where was she going? I knew it! We watched a movie months before that ended up with someone moving to Mexico to start a new life. "Well, that's one way to start over," she said sarcastically.

For the next hour, I played out the scenario at least 10 times, which usually involved her with sombreros and shaking maracas looking to start a new life. About two hours later, I heard, "Christa, phone," and my dad handed it to me.

"What time should I pick you up tomorrow?" It was my mom! I could barely talk.

"I have your sunglasses," was all I could mumble.

"How about after school?" my mom answered and thanked me for picking up the sunglasses.

"See you then, love you," she said, and I hung up the phone.

What? She didn't leave us? I was going to see her again! I didn't dare ask my dad what happened but grabbed some Kleenex and then went back to my room. So, all that time I made up some story in my mind that wasn't true! I assumed she was gone. Had I watched too many movies? Those hours after she left felt like an eternity and my imagination ran wild. Now as I look back, I can create a new movie.

Pre-suffering

Worry engulfed me just thinking about something tragic happening; from someone dying, getting injured, or losing all the pictures on my phone. No matter what was going on, when the phone rang, for example, I would go to the worst-case scenario, imagining scenarios that never happened, or if they did, all the worrying only wasted time and denied my enjoyment of the present.

"I'm just a worrier!" was my excuse but I was just used to telling myself that. I would let my imagination go to all sorts of places, making up crazy stories. Once you're aware of this, instead of repeating that things never work out, ask yourself, ***"What if everything works out?"***

I started doing this every time worry set in and my automatic thoughts were *OMG the sky is falling down.* Now see how that feels. The more you do it the more it reprograms your mind and breaks that habit. This is the key to staying present and living in a state of joy, not fear.

Useless Guilt

Going to our trailer was our summer getaway from the city. Swimming was one of the highlights of our trip. One sunny afternoon, I swam out to a floating raft and sprawled out to tan. Kids loved to climb on the raft, jump off and show their latest swan dive!

There was a group of cousins who made it to my tanning spot, but yes, I knew I had to share. As much as I hated being splashed, it was fun to watch the belly flops.

The group swam back, and a little girl in a pretty pink bathing suit was obviously tired. I almost told her to rest first, but she was going to be with her cousins, so I flipped over to even out my tan.

The beach was starting to clear, and so was the sun so I braved the chilly water and headed to the beach. "Hey, did you see a little girl with a pink bathing suit?" a random stranger yelled.

"Yes, on the raft with her cousins."

"She probably went back to the trailer," he shouted to the other adults.

As I reached the shore, I saw my nightmare, the little girl in the pink bathing suit being pulled out of the water. I ran to the convenience store, called the ambulance, and lead them to the beach. She was whisked away. In my innocent mind, I figured she was going to be ok because the ambulance was there. The next day, there was a short memo stating she passed away, thanking everyone involved in looking for her.

My heart sank and my mind started to spin. I ran back to the trailer and told my mom. I cried because I felt guilty. I should have said something to the little girl, I knew she was tired.

I was a faceless part of this story. No counselling and it definitely wasn't something we talked about.

I originally took this part out of the book but was later told to put it back in to show how we can hold onto guilt that we don't own. That's the true message. Guilt serves no purpose, and if anyone feels stuck, it's important to get help and talk about it because no matter how hard you try, it doesn't magically disappear. Once I dealt with it, I was able to see it for what it was, let go of any responsibility I created in my mind and finally found peace.

Ultimately, in my life, I learned to surrender to what I couldn't control. I couldn't control giving life or having life taken away. I couldn't control others' actions, but I could control how I reacted. I have no influence on the weather, or if a plane is going to be canceled, or if I was meant to be tall, have blue eyes, or if someone was going to love me. And trust me, I tried. Once I learned to accept that I'm not the ruler of the world, I was happier.

Every day, there are people who are going to be pissed off, treat others badly, and overall, have different morals than I have. So why am I so surprised when it happens? I accepted that I'll encounter all of this and that life isn't fair. Whose standards determine what's fair anyway? I can change my views, opinions, actions, attitude, thoughts, and words. The rest is going to be what it will be. Once this hit home, I lived with more peace of mind and focused on what I could control.

Declutter your mess, declutter your mind.

"I'll be one minute!" I said as I was checking every nook and cranny for my ring that I hid in a special place so it would be safe, but now I couldn't flipping find it! We were going out

> "Simplicity, less stuff, less work, less expense equals more money, more time, and more joy. Less equals more."
> UNKNOWN

for dinner, so I squeezed through my closet to get the one pair of acceptable jeans I could be seen wearing in public, only to get stuck. I found those old frumpy ones and that bright orange t-shirt that I only wore on Halloween. That was it! I tore apart my closet and anything I was saving because I thought I might fit back into it, or it would come back in fashion. I put it in a bag, including the ugly orange T-shirt. Wow, I could actually see what I had, and I found three pairs of jeans!

I went to grab some boxes from the storage room. There were bins labeled Rob's stuff, vases I dusted just in case I needed them, oh and a random old bread maker. I grabbed a pen to mark the boxes, only to find the first three were dry as a desert. I managed to find a half-sharpened pencil. Broken pencils are pointless. Why are we keeping these? I took them all out and now our "junk drawer" was a drawer we could store things that worked (I won't get into the number of dead batteries, not to mention the pile of keys and miscellaneous cords to nothing).

Guess what the bonus was? I found other things that I hid away in a secret place that, of course, I forgot where I put it. Jackpot! Kids, I love the 3,000 Valentine's Day cards you got

Skip The Pain, Experience The Pleasure

since junior kindergarten, but I promise you, you won't even remember these people, and definitely, they won't be your sweetheart, so it's OK to let them go.

Vases are meant to be filled. Clothes are meant to be worn. If I wasn't going to use them, I could let them fulfil their purpose with somebody else. I looked back and felt like a huge weight was lifted off my shoulders. It was like I decluttered my mind.

For Christmas, some of my team members got me this beautiful basket of lotions that looked amazing on the side of my bathtub. Oh yeah, these were something else I ended up just dusting them because it didn't take long before they became rancid. So first, I'm sorry to the guys who got me these, and my message is to just use up those damn lotions, loofahs, and gifts you receive. If you don't use it, pass it on. I had to stop saving things for special occasions. Today is special. A rich life is full of memories, not things that collect dust and break. Experiences live forever. When I look back, I remember experiences, not things.

Summary of Insights

- You have no control over your past, but you do have control over how you can learn from it. Let go of the suffering and live in the present.

- Worrying about the future is only an overactive imagination.

- Focus on the present before the present becomes your past. Remember to ask yourself, "What if everything works out?"

- Guilt is a useless emotion. You are not responsible for everything that goes wrong. By hanging onto guilt, you're holding yourself back from healing.

- Speak up when you are hurting. Going through anything that feels traumatic (and that is individualized) needs to be dealt with instead of sweeping it under the rug.

- Everything has a purpose, if it's not being used, let someone else use it and fulfil its purpose. The best weight to take off is the clutter around you. Trust me, you'll feel lighter and save years of your life trying to hunt for things.

Chapter 6

VITALITY AND VIGOR

Most people don't value it until they lose it.

Rare Disease Should Not Be So Rare

Why was Lyme disease so rare? Back when I was 14 and camping, I remember that disgusting tick that had the Jaws of Life gripped into me as we tried to rip it out with pliers. "Gross," I said as I was on my way to the nearest clinic. We thought I was having an allergic reaction because this red bull's-eye ring formed where the dead head was still stuck.

"You have Lyme disease," the doctor said after using tweezers to remove the head and taking some blood work.

He gave me some antibiotics, but I had no idea how serious it was. I barely made it through one week of the antibiotics, but the red circle started to fade at least. Not a sexy look, especially since I was a young teen.

My body was so sore, and this was only the beginning. Years later, after suffering each day with body pain, brain fog, flare-ups, and more, I couldn't find a doctor who would take this seriously because it was so long ago. Our normal tests won't pick up if you have Lyme disease because the levels they're checking won't show up in the mainstream tests. Now I have a chronic advanced case of Lyme disease.

I let it go for 30 years then I found a doctor in Germany who did some tests and confirmed Lyme disease and offered me treatment. This was going to cost thousands of dollars. I was planning to go, but unfortunately, I was devastated by being scammed out of the money I needed to go through treatment.

Too Smart to Be Scammed, or So I Thought

While I was preparing to go for treatment in Germany, I found out I was a victim of a highly intricate scam that cost me $53,000. I was totally broken; I was usually the one warning others about scams. I worked with the special crimes unit for months and I was able to recover $24,000. "It happens to people exactly like you, these criminals are professionals," the police told me.

Now I didn't have the money I was going to use for treatment in Germany. I constantly blamed myself, but I'm sharing this extremely painful lesson with the hope that it might help someone else. The point is not to blame yourself because these scammers are so skilled at what they do. It's a form of brainwashing, and no one is immune. Unfortunately, it's so easy for people to pretend to be someone they're not, even down to the tiniest details. I did have some suspicions, so I looked it up and this company seemed to be legit. As I continued to research, there were no red flags. They had the skills to copy an exact website, and new every detail right down to the security questions. I finally kept following my intuition and pressed on the "Contact Us" button. Nothing happened. I left the website, and looked it up again following a different link, only to find the right one and yes, the information was there when I pressed the same button. Thank goodness I did, because the police said these exact criminals have scammed people out of their life savings, and some even lost their houses.

Coincidently, there was a fundraiser for a lady who was also scammed. She was about my age, intelligent, and I knew there was a reason I found out about this fundraiser to bring awareness, so I had to go to support her. Her courage to share her story gave me the courage to share mine. I never did make it for treatment but there was more to come.

New symptoms started like a magic show I wanted to shut the curtain on. Breathing became a chore, and I ended up with a new collection of inhalers. My body had more tricks as I became the ultimate allergy magnet, with hives taking over my body. It felt like hot oatmeal being poured on me.

I was constantly freezing and exhausted, and it turned out I had hypothyroidism. So, they put me on medication. It was like my immune system went on strike!

Skip The Pain, Experience The Pleasure

My heartbeat was like a wild drummer when I found out there was a name for it: Wolfe Parkinson White Syndrome. I guess I hoped for a miraculous transformation into a supercharged version of myself but that wasn't going to occur during this magic act yet.

I went from one specialist to another, playing a game of prescription roulette. "Hmm, you've got something serious going on." As if I needed confirmation of my deteriorating sanity! As I kept stuffing things down, the sicker I got. My body couldn't take much more. I coined it "emotional constipation" when I was unable to deal with my emotions.

Even though after my car accident I was diagnosed by my doctor with fibromyalgia, it seemed to be swept under the rug. Having said that, I clearly had all the symptoms; I had specific pain in certain parts of my body when touched, as well as generalized pain, fatigue, and more but again, was this just a sneaky part of Lyme disease? Was it all in my head?

Fast forward to today. It turns out that both Lyme disease and Fibromyalgia are indeed legitimate conditions. It's like the scientific community collectively said, "Hey, we might have dismissed these too quickly."

So here I was, caught in the crossfire of what seemed to be a comical medical debate, although there was no humor for me. It seems as if no one knows how to handle both of these conditions yet everyone seems to have an opinion about them. At least I can find solace in knowing that I'm not alone. We can band together, armed with weird symptoms and a prayer for a cure. At that time, I didn't realize that these were only some of the battles I was going to fight.

Puzzle Piece

The lights were blinding, and my muscles ached as if I had done a full day's workout! (I wish I had.) "She's awake," a nurse said, and my husband grabbed a cloth to wipe my sweaty forehead.

This was the beginning, or maybe a continuation, of this mysterious disease. I was a puzzle piece. Over four years, my overall health had deteriorated. It started with seizures, trips in the ambulance, and ended in the intensive care unit too many times to count.

I started falling, having weird hallucinations, hearing incredibly high-pitched noises, and experiencing unpredictable muscle spasms and shaking. I would forget things that I would normally know, kind of like a photographic memory that didn't develop.

My white blood cells plummeted, and I was sent urgently for a bone marrow biopsy. The pain was unbearable, but I didn't have a choice. The memories of my late husband going through the same journey brought back immense fear and sorrow.

We tried several different treatments. One of them caused me to have paralysis from the waist down, and I was slowly going blind from one of the medications. I wouldn't let anything stop me, so I became a warrior. I would travel two hours to go to my daughter's dance recital or my children's basketball tournaments, so I had some of the dads carry me up the stairs while sitting on my walker. I was blessed to have so much support.

I travelled to different hospitals and continued with more tests, including countless blood tests, spinal taps, ultrasounds, and pet scans (scans of your entire body) as my body started to shut down. I clearly remember the pain of having 32 electrodes stuck to my scalp to watch my neurological waves. I was also videotaped during the process, so I didn't dare pick my nose; I mean these were permanent records!

For a short time, I started to slip into what seemed to be a catatonic state; I couldn't move or talk, although I could hear absolutely everything. A reminder to those who cross my path, it was so inappropriate to talk about your dates or drama and complain about working a double shift or other co-workers. Remember, even though a patient can't respond, often they can hear you. Would you talk about these things around your loved one?

Intubation

It just became too hard, and my body checked out. My scariest memory is when I heard the mumbling of people talking about me and then I could see them putting oxygen masks on me. I was very confused, but at the same time, I knew exactly what was going on.

As they were intubating me, everything went black. Then it was dark, kind of like being in space. All that pain I felt slipped away as I continued in this darkness. Suddenly, my body was engulfed with a feeling of total love. There were these white, glowing light figures starting to come closer, and I felt more love. As I basked in the glory of this feeling, I could start to clearly see the world as we know it and everyone in it. That was my turning point, I felt this pulling sensation then I made a choice and drifted away from the most beautiful light and love I had ever experienced because I still had to fulfil my purpose, whatever that may be. I knew this love would always be there, but I made the decision to return to my body.

At that moment, I felt the hard bed underneath me and a rigid painful structure down my throat. I started slowly wiggling a finger until I heard, "She's starting to wake up!"

A flood of doctors came to me, took out the tube, and kept oxygen on me, but I still could remember the sensation of that loving feeling, despite my bodily pain. I had no sense of the time or date. This was four days after one of my largest episodes. Was it a dream? Was it the pain meds? Was it a near-death experience? Does it matter? I don't interpret it; I just know my experience. This was just one of the many secrets I kept so that others wouldn't think my health was that serious.

And who would've guessed? Yup, life had gotten so bizarre that I looked forward to the smells of the cleaning chemicals from the housekeepers. The orderlies who stayed with me during my isolation periods brightened my days. They saw beyond the medical equipment and treated me like a fellow human being. We discussed everything from the weather to the latest movies. Those unsung heroes made a significant impact, even though they often went unnoticed.

Mystery Solved: Diagnoses

So, there I was, back in the intensive care unit, surrounded by neurologists who burst into the room exclaiming, "Eureka! I've found the missing piece of the puzzle!"

Let's rewind a few months earlier. I had this neurology specialist who decided to send my blood work away, searching for some elusive rare disease. I called him my earth angel because he confirmed I had something called Anti-GAD. Now, normal levels are under five but mine? Oh no, it decided to skyrocket to a whopping 250 (finding out later it was approximately 450)! I couldn't quite grasp the details he was throwing at me, but tears were streaming down my face, and my heart was pounding like a drum because finally, I had that missing puzzle piece I had been praying for all this time!

Now, what on earth is Anti-GAD? Well, it turns out it's a rare disease that robs you of GABA. Normally we all produce Gaba but because of my Anti-Gad, I don't produce enough. It messes with your fine motor skills, making simple tasks like typing, writing, or even zipping up zippers difficult. It also messes with your brain, affecting your memory and ability to operate a phone, speak coherently, or even find the right words. It's utterly frustrating! As if that wasn't enough, did I mention I'm at a higher risk for hypothyroidism, diabetes, and cancer now? Welcome to my new reality! Fear of my future took over and I had a hard time keeping up hope.

Vitality and Vigor

There are many other rare diseases like hidden planets. I hope that sharing mine will inspire other doctors to consider thinking outside of the box and to lean on others who may have more expertise. Even then, if there's even an inkling that it could be something other than the normal diagnosis, go with that hunch. Do that extra test. For me, that hunch saved my life.

Because of this rare disease, Anti-GAD, it was easier to find a needle in a haystack than a doctor in this field. I was given a "time frame". As my husband and I drove home, we both balled, mainly due to fear. After the initial shock and emotions, as soon as we got home, I made a list, including our will and everything else I should have already done, I mean it's not like I didn't know. I had a will, but it wasn't close to being updated, and we left no rock unturned.

That was heavy, but it was one of the Ah-Ha moments that I had to share. Do you know why? Because I already talked about this to someone, and that night, she had a conversation with her partner, and they made their wills. "That was painless!" So, I helped one person, and this is why I'm sharing this.

My testing included spinal taps and different meds, and I was on IVIG (intravenous Immunoglobulin) treatment for three years. I would be in the hospital for nine hours, only to be so drugged up that I would do crazy things, like changing in the living room instead of my bedroom. I had to get my dressing from my port changed weekly, and it often peeled off my skin. I ended up with a bacterial infection in my bloodstream and symptoms of meningitis. Back to the hospital I went. It felt like a merry-go-round.

Skip The Pain, Experience The Pleasure

People kept telling me I was strong but to be transparent, I wasn't always. I almost gave up, many times. On my way home, we went through a drive-through. When asked what I would like to order, I said, "A large coffee with two milks," and in my mind, I continued, "With a side order of a will to live." The pain almost broke me, but I held on. Sometimes, one second at a time, but I did it.

You see, when you hear hooves, what is the first thing that comes to your mind? Usually a horse, no one looks for a zebra. This is a great way to think of diagnoses that don't fit in the regular box.

My real challenge was to change how I *felt* about myself, my diagnosis, my identity, and my life. The point of a diagnosis is just that. An illness is not your new name, it's part of your life story. There's a quote I use often:

> "I rather have been remembered for overcoming my tragedies, than being a victim of them."
> — UNKNOWN

Masks, Online Tasks, Hug Me, Don't Ask!

Speaking about being sick, Covid-19 was a virus that became a pandemic and turned the world upside down.

This chapter was done, edited, and then the universe figured I experienced everything else in this book, so now let's give her Covid! I found out how many paper cuts I had after using hand sanitizer so much!

Vitality and Vigor

I woke up on a Tuesday at 3 am, feeling like an elephant was sitting on me. Every part of my body hurt, my throat and lungs were on fire, and I started throwing up blood. And yes, I tested positive. Everyone has different experiences with Covid, some much worse and some not as serious.

A global pandemic stole millions from life-long careers and family businesses. It didn't matter what your name badge said, Covid didn't discriminate.

My kids sat in front of a screen instead of being in school. I picked up the phone to talk to my doctor instead of going in to see them. Our grocery bill doubled, and we would have to wait hours in line only to find many shelves empty. Turning on the news, I saw people start fighting over toilet paper!

When asked if Covid-19 was serious, one of the craziest answers I heard was when all the casinos and churches were closed and Heaven and Hell agreed on the same thing, then it's serious. I guess this was some attempt to provide humor for some trying to deal with it in their own way.

My great-aunt died from Covid, and there are so many stories I've heard but the one that stuck with me the most was about a father dying in the ICU and his wife only being able to see and talk to him through a phone the nurses held. He died without the ability to hold his wife's hand. There were no longer job descriptions, everyone worked from their heart. My son made these ear savers for people wearing masks, hoping to provide some relief and donated them to various hospitals. We were in different parts globally but were all fighting the same war against the COVID-19 pandemic.

Summary of Insights

- **Health is never guaranteed. Value it.**

- **Even if it sounds like a horse, it could be a zebra.**

- **Be thankful for those who make a difference in your life. It's usually the ones who are the most overlooked.**

- **Mental and physical illness doesn't discriminate, whether you see it or not.**

- **A global pandemic can change the way the world functions. Remember what it was like to not have freedom? What turned out to be your new "normal", and what lessons have we learned? I learned that the world is more connected than we thought. Yes, it's a small world after all.**

Chapter 7

GIVE UP HOPE

HOPE: Heck Over Pleasing Everyone

Who Am I Now?

I was waiting to go to the airport when I got the call. It was my boss. I already had a feeling this wasn't going to be just a friendly check-up. I was already off work for a few years and was waiting to go to a treatment center in another country. They held my job as long as they could.

"I'm so sorry, but we can't hold the job any longer." I thanked them for the tremendous opportunity to work for them and was grateful for all the efforts they made for me.

I hung up the phone, and tears streamed down my face. It wasn't the "news" that bothered me the most, it was thinking about how I would now respond to the question, "So what do you do?"

I immediately realized I had no idea who I was because my identity was my job and my passion, but now I was left feeling empty. Fear set in, as my identity at that moment seemed to be gone. I kissed my husband goodbye and walked on the plane. As much as I tried not to think about it, the more I thought about it! So, I can identify with those who felt they just lost their identity when it was wrapped up in what job they did.

I didn't need any extra reminders that time and health is not guaranteed. I used to be a type A personality who loved to host parties, dance, and embrace my work with a passion! I was so far from being that person now. I had three sides, the always smiling, the fun and crazy side, and the side you never want to see (or at least I would try to hide it). Like I said, who was I now?

The most horrible thing isn't losing a job, crashing your car, or hearing a dire diagnosis. We live or we die. We can starve our souls as we kill ourselves replaying horrific things and suffering while preparing for the future that never comes as planned. The true disaster is living the life in your mind and missing the one right in front of you.

My Ah-Ha Moment

I was back in the hospital lying in bed for about six weeks with no mirror and I could barely see my reflection in the window,

Give Up Hope

but that didn't seem to matter. I really didn't care at this point; I was very sick. Finally, I was rolled into an actual bathroom and glanced at myself in the mirror. I barely recognized my own reflection. My bones were showing, and I had more chin hairs than a monkey. This is when self-talk showed its power. I looked in that mirror and then looked away. I couldn't tell her anything, well, except maybe to wax or shave, but that was my limit. It was because I accepted myself as this sick, ugly, weak, hairy person. It was when everything in life was coming my way. I figured, at this point, I was probably in the wrong lane!

Then I had someone say to me, "Wow you look better!" I thought maybe they hit their head or were on some strong meds, but they saw through the chin hairs and saw me sitting up in a chair, actually looking alive not laying there like a wet noodle.

They saw me, not what I thought they should be seeing. This was a huge turning point because it started me on my road to self-acceptance. One amazing nurse used a string to help cut those wiggly hairs, then I texted my mom to bring in tweezers and a small mirror. People began telling me how I inspired them, and as I looked around, I saw people who were much sicker than I was, but I saw beauty in their suffering and felt joyful when I saw any bit of progress. I was filled with gratitude. Heck, I was using my hands and could (almost) use those tweezers. Yes, tweezers were such a small thing, but they became symbolic of progress and self-acceptance. They were encouraging because they saw me coming back to life. That was kindness.

It's Okay to Give Up Hope

Heck **O**ver **P**leasing **E**veryone

I was lost and it seemed like I was the only one who felt like I didn't have a place in this world. It turned out it was linked to the feeling of a loss of hope. That secret place that no one wants to admit, I know I didn't. I found out it was fine! I learned it was ok to give up hope! I sat upright in bed, and it instantly came to me. Hope can stand for: Heck Over Pleasing Everyone. I tried to do everything for everyone else until I ended up spiraling down and I couldn't do it. I was empty. I wanted to stay in bed, throw the sheets over my head and say enough. With all the pressures of the world, and more so the pressures I put on myself, it was easy to feel like I simply existed to please others.

I used to carry around this whip and used it any time I was asked to do something, but really wanted to say no. One thing I found is that when I truly said **h**eck **o**ver **p**leasing **e**veryone and taking care of myself, that's when the meaning changed to **h**old **o**n, **p**ain **e**nds. My value is not determined by what others think; I started to focus on what was working and not working in my life and took small actions to change it. I had a choice of what road to stay on. I almost missed the exit because I was blinded by overworking, overdoing, and over-pleasing others. It wasn't an overnight transformation, but I did find hope! These fires inside me made me realize I want to inspire people. I want someone to look at me and say, ***"Because of you, I didn't give up hope."***

Woo-woo meds?

I was done with being pricked, poked, and prodded over every part of me and having meds that would make me feel paralyzed or blind. I didn't fall into the "set procedure" category. Yeah, I needed to find another route. I figured the doctors were making good money to figure out what they could do for this rare disease, so I would let them have that job and look for something else.

It's as if conventional medicine is the same restaurant you go to all the time and order from the same menu. It's pretty standard. But holistic healing is like checking out different restaurants with endless food choices. So, when it comes to dealing with pain, both emotional and physical, you might try some new ingredients. I thought about all that woo-woo stuff that I wasn't sure if I believed in, but I also didn't believe in chocolate milk in my ice cappuccino but dang, why did it take me so long to figure out that little delight?

So, I grabbed a new list of restaurants and flipped through the menus. I found energy work is like ghost peppers that use the power of your body's energy to help heal with just enough kick. Reflexology is like a foot massage on steroids, stimulating pressure points in your feet connected to different parts of your body to boost your overall well-being. Reiki is like a hug from the universe, using energy to help you heal, reduce pain, and find balance. Access bars are 32 points on your head that could change your life, or at least give you a great head massage! Ironically, they're the same points as the electrodes, coincidence? I think not. I also did acupuncture, and massage, and became more open to other healing modalities. A specialist studied light therapy, so under his supervision, I also tried that, and it worked.

Mother Nature, the sneaky healer! I was in agony, ready to unleash a wild scream. But instead, I stepped outside, barefoot, felt a plop on my head. Thank goodness it was just rain! Little did I know, that drop would change everything.

I looked up, a giant tree shielding me from the downpour. Nature's way of saying, "I got you covered!"

So, next time I felt pain and overwhelm, no more screaming into the void. Just a chat with a tree, some deep breaths, and voila! Mind and body found peace faster than melting ice cream.

Nature, the unsung hero, always at my doorstep. Cheers to Mother Nature, the world's finest healer - no degree needed!

Our bodies and emotions are intertwined. I wanted to be nice and alert for a job interview, so I chugged my coffee on the way. As soon as I got there, the coffee seemed to travel through me, and I searched for the closest bathroom.

That's funny, why is there ice in the sinks? I thought. Then a shocked male walked out. Yes, I was in the men's bathroom and obviously didn't know what a urinal looked like. My heart was beating faster than a race car, and I started sweating as if it was going to be a wet t-shirt contest. I reached for my anxiety pill. It was in the other purse. As I walked out, my name was called and as I sat down, that shocked man was there!

Give Up Hope

"Christa, right? I believe we briefly met," he said with a smirk. That was it, I already showed I was incompetent before I started. My voice swelled and I could barely squeak out, yeah sorry about that" as I was still crossing my legs because I didn't get to go!

Don't worry, the signs aren't clear, it happens all the time, then gave me a grin and changed the subject back to job related questions. Well, I had no problem answering the question, "How did you handle an unexpected problem". "Well, I came into this interview, so I faced my fear head on!"

No more questions, I got the job. As I walked out, I took my time to double check I went into the right washroom. I splashed water on my face and started to laugh, as I began to calm down.

As soon as the interview was over, I wasn't worried, and my anxiety dropped. The root cause was worry! Yes, sometimes I did have anxiety, but I needed to follow my intuition and dig a little bit deeper before grabbing some medication. Oh, and I double-checked what washroom I was in, and yes, had to ask a friend why there was ice. If you're reading this, and don't know, I'm not going to be the one to spoil it for you.

The point is to look at the root cause of the symptom, try any other coping skills instead of slapping a Band-Aid on it by using medication.

I started to become laser-focused on what my body was doing, and often I could catch some subtle changes right at the beginning of tremors, spasms, headaches and zoning out. Then, like a private investigator, I would look for what triggered it. At times it seemed like everything around me was amplified, the lights seemed blinding, or a sudden noise could set me off. Heck, between someone crunching on a breadstick, with the TV on in the background, I felt sorry for the person who suddenly passed gas at the same time!

Who would have thought that once I looked at what I felt was really the culprit, I was able to practice different techniques and this way, able to proactively kick illness to the curb instead of waiting to deal with the symptoms.

You would be shocked how an illness or symptoms of them would pop up right before making a huge decision, or even how past traumas can rear their ugly head and invade our immune system.

Since then, I checked in with how I felt both physically and emotionally and slowly saw a connection. It was like adding that secret spice to my well-being recipe. It tasted amazing!

I started trading supplements for medication, keeping my doctor in the loop. I already had a background in nutrition but expanded my studies in natural medicine and herbalism. Who would have thought that dandelions had numerous health benefits, instead of being a pesky weed? Or eating raw garlic could boost your immune system and so much more rather than just keeping vampires away! And using your gut isn't just about using your intuition; it can be the root of all evil if it's unbalanced and unhealthy. The journey didn't end there. I studied and became a practitioner in several of these modalities, and I dove head-first into Intuitive Healing. Why? Because I wanted to use my newfound knowledge to help others.

Give Up Hope

A skill before pills is what I learned. I only focused on how I could get some relief. I had less and less pain the more I did this. Now to be transparent, I couldn't do it all the time. I would cry, scream, and punch my daughter's stuffed animal Squishmallows (oops sorry), but I did this less often. And by the way, no Squishmallow was harmed in any way, shape, or form during this process. Cross my heart.

What I put in my body was essential. I went vegetarian and gluten-free at first but gradually introduced meat and I have a small tolerance to gluten. If I grabbed a bag or box of food, looked at the ingredients and saw it was a mile long with words I couldn't pronounce, it went back on the shelf. Now, I call it the 80/20 rule. 80% of the time, I ate delicious, nutritional food, and 20% of the time, I ate what I craved. As soon as you say you can't have it, the more you want it. Once in a while, I ate chocolate and carrots with no guilt. I went to a qualified natural health store and took the supplements my body needed. Creams, crystals, prayers, and getting a service dog were all part of this new discovery as well.

We're constantly changing. First, our bodies literally change hundreds of times. Our skin has fallen off enough to make thousands of you, our skeleton has changed, and science says that essentially, most of our body's cells are replaced every seven to 10 years, which is weird, so we really can be a new person—well, at least skin deep.

Now, I'm not saying you should ditch conventional medicine; it definitely has its place. But when it comes to truly healing from the inside out, you might want to give holistic methods a try. Who knows? As wacky as it sounded to me, once I

Skip The Pain, Experience The Pleasure

opened up to it, I had more options, like new ingredients to try. My journey to wellness turned into a delicious meal.

You know what I found out was the cheapest medicine? Laughter! I had a few people over and started getting into a deep conversation. My husband texted me, but my fingers started cramping so I tried the voice to text. It worked, except with autocorrect!

Darrin: How are you feeling? Do you want me to bring anything home?

Me: You're the best, I'm pretty sore so maybe some lesbian? I have a few people over so it would be a big help.

Darrin: How is a lesbian going to help? Maybe I shouldn't ask.

Me: Lebanese you know…food! Damn autocorrect.

Darrin: Sure…

I started laughing so hard I was spitting and maybe snorting a little bit! All I could do was show everyone else the phone. The laugh was contagious like a yawn. That was it, the whole group started laughing. The feeling of the deep conversation turned into a feel-good state, and it reminded us not to take ourselves so seriously. From then on, I focused on bringing as much humor into my life as possible, and yes, it's one of the best medicines. So, I guess now I'm a fully-fledged member of the Woo-Woo community!

Give Up Hope

Living with pain and trying to be happy is a bit like trying to dance the Tango with a bowling ball strapped to your foot. It's not exactly easy, but hey, if you can pull it off, you'll be a master of both pain management and ballroom dancing!

All jokes aside, living with pain is no laughing matter, but it's important to find ways to keep your spirits up and stay positive. When I'm having a flare-up, it feels like it will never end, and that's when I must remind myself, "This too shall pass," and it always does, sometimes quicker than others, but it always passes. There are always things you can do to find a bit more happiness in life. So, don't forget to dance like nobody's watching.

Summary of Insights

- It's okay to give up hope. Sometimes you have to scream, Heck Over Pleasing Everyone so you can feel, Hold On - Pain Ends.

- Appreciate that people see the progress you make, and that's the true beauty.

- Take responsibility for what you can control, and keep your mind open to new things, even if it's looking outside the box—it doesn't matter if you think it's "woo-who, wacky, or weird". All medicine started off like that.

- Don't underestimate the healing powers of nature.

- Living with chronic pain doesn't mean you have to limit your life!

- Find any way to bring happiness into your day, even if it's an autocorrect message (and please no hate mail, blame autocorrect!)

- Turn it around. Instead of focusing on what you can't do, make a joke out of it, accept it, and add some zest instead of being depressed.

Chapter 8

WAIT FOR IT!

Asking WAIT- What Am I Thinking and Why Am I Talking?

I Made a Decision That Changed My Life

What were the secrets to starting on the road to recovery? It was changing my mindset. My words, beliefs, thoughts, and behaviors all equaled my reality. That's right, I choose my reality!

This was it, I had to change it from, *I'm never going to get better* and all those thoughts about giving up to, *I'm going to heal; I'm getting better every day. This is my final choice and decision.* Once I made that decision, all other decisions were already set on the right path. The best part of it was I didn't have to make it again. There wasn't any magic pill even though I looked for one. I felt as if I had a voicemail that said, "I'm out of my mind, will be back in 10 minutes!"

Whenever a thought that brought up daggers of painful memories came up, I had to choose to think differently. How I thought, felt, and believed became my reality. I became my biggest bully, simply because of the way I would talk to myself. When the difficult times added up, it became harder, but not impossible. I thought back to the millions of decisions I made throughout the years. White? Sage? Green? Strapless? These decisions were so important when picking out my prom dress.

Dang, why didn't I make the decision to invest my babysitting money in Google, Amazon, sanitizer, or air fryers back then? Every day, every hour, every second there's a choice. As I grab my coffee, I have a flashback about how many decisions I've made, good or bad, right, or wrong, suntan lotion or oil, that all determined my next move, even if that meant an embarrassing sunburn.

When I realized that, it scared the heebie-jeebies out of me! I was paralyzed by fear of making a wrong choice. This goes for all the decisions I've made in the past that shaped who I am today, what I've achieved, my health, my loved ones, and whether I'm in jail or not.

> "In every single thing you do, you're constantly making a decision that will choose a direction. Your life is a result of each choice."
> UNKNOWN

But how did I know if I was making the right decisions? I did research and listened to my gut, and when that didn't work, I tried rock paper scissors.

My emotions became my alarm. My life was only as good as I felt it was.

From everything I've gone through, I finally realized that paying attention to my emotions is no joke and I had to start taking it seriously if I really wanted to change my life. I used to just let my feelings run wild, and the next thing you know, I was knee-deep in a pit of sadness, depression, and anxiety. I can't just brush it off and hope it goes away. I end up reacting usually out of anger instead of responding calmly.

That's why I use the acronym WAIT, which stands for "What Am I Thinking?" Whenever I start feeling even a bit of depression sneaking in, I ask myself this question to check my thoughts and see if they're true or if I'm just ruminating over something that happened or spiraling out of control. I consciously run through the drama and chaos that is in my mind and then challenge myself to ask, "What do I *want* to think and feel instead?"

I've realized that how I think, and talk becomes my reality, and I don't want my reality to be full of limiting beliefs that hold me back from what I really want to do. Sometimes, I would just simply say, "Eeny, Meeny, Miny, Moe," and the universe would give me a nudge in the right direction.

I returned home from my hospital stay; everything was set up for me but none of that seemed to matter. I still had to use a walker and had a difficult time speaking and dressing myself. I pretty much lived in my bed. Was this going to be my life? I had to realize that accepting help wasn't a weakness. I had to get honest, real honest.

I needed to break the cycle. So, I stumbled into my closet and thought about grabbing some jogging pants. I mean, I could use the excuse that I was sick, so it didn't matter what I wore. Hell, I could stay in a bathrobe 24 hours a day, not quite the sexy look I used to have.

I grabbed some jeans and a simple sweater; I was always freezing. Forget the bra, a tank top would do; I mean, little steps first. I felt like a contortionist trying to wiggle myself into these clothes. I stood up a little straighter, wet my hair and put some chapstick on. I smiled and felt excited as if I had some big surprise! I grabbed my walker and made myself take small, slow steps out of the bedroom. I saw the look on my family's faces; they thought I looked like a bomb! Seriously, a simple outfit after staying in pajamas changed my reality. It felt as if I was in some power clothes, and when I looked better, I behaved differently. Was I sore? Yes! Would I have been sore lying down? Yes!

Sometimes I have bad nights, mornings, or afternoons but I don't let it take over my whole day or week. It may mean I need to rest or reach out, but I had to learn when to say no. My friends accepted me and remembered when I was charismatic, captivating, and sometimes corny but those days seemed light years away. I'm slowly getting back to that!

I Learned to Set the Bar Low

I remember getting set up to start my journey toward being limber, flexible, and loose. As I looked at my walker, it was anything but alluring. The pure fact of being able to get around was all it took to become stimulated. My kids loved taking me for rides. I did graduate to a cane but when I started to spin down feeling helpless, I would spin the cane in a tantalizing way, which would always bring a smile to my husband's face. I had to consciously turn things around.

I had to stop being so self-conscious, especially with the way I spoke. My family coined the phrase "Christa-ism". It always made us laugh when I said everything was a thingy or asked for a glass of paper, no refrigerator, and no water! Ding! I knew I would get it eventually. Then I asked them to get me water, but not in the blue cup and we don't own any blue cups. I could say a sentence and leave out words, and as they looked at me like I learned a new language, I simply said, "You know what I mean" and at times, we turned it into a game of charades. The best part is they weren't laughing at me, they were laughing with me. It was all about how I was going to perceive it. Heck, it was funny, especially when it turned into a game of guess what I'm saying.

Skip The Pain, Experience The Pleasure

> "So, if we want to change some aspect of our reality, we have to think, feel, and act in new ways; we have to "be" different in terms of our responses to experiences. We have to "become" someone else. We have to create a new state of mind ... we need to observe a new outcome with that new mind."
>
> JOE DISPENZA

That's when I changed my focus and looked for ways to feel good. A lot of times, it was when my family felt good, but I couldn't let external factors determine how I felt. Think of it like an egg, if it cracks on the outside, it's broken but if it starts cracking from the inside, it means there's life. Great things happen from the inside. I definitely felt cracked but when my emotions started to drag me down, I looked inside and focused on anything that would bring happiness into my life. Like any habit, I had to practice changing my thoughts from being negative or judgmental and bringing my emotions up over and over until it became subconscious, like a knee-jerk response.

Flashing back to when I was 16, I got off the bus when a couple of guys asked if I wanted to play chess with them after school. I wasn't used to getting attention from boys, so just as I was feeling flattered, they continued saying, "Yeah, we need a flat surface to play chess on." Yes, I wasn't blessed up top, but it wasn't until that moment that I became self-conscious.

Flipping through every magazine, I saw women doing weight-lifting programs that seemed to be exactly what my stick figure body needed. I went for the first time, and every part of me ached. As much as I wanted to quit, I didn't; I was determined to finish the program. After the first week, I noticed there was some sort of muscle there. "We must, we must, and we must increase our bust!" was the chant the ladies said as we giggled, working on our pecks. Did I become voluptuous after a few weeks? No, but I noticed I stood up straighter and built some confidence. I kept doing it and by the end of the month, it wasn't just obvious that I built some muscle, I self-confidently felt firmer.

To wrap it all up, my mindset influenced everything. From the moment I wake up until the moment I crawl into bed, everything in-between is up to me. This includes my emotions, my thoughts, my perception, my assumptions and whether I respond or react. In every moment, in every day.

Where Your Focus Goes, Your Energy Grows

It was as simple as when I was driving home from the hospital about two hours away and had to go to the bathroom so badly because of all the IVs. About a half hour in, I remembered we forgot to lock the front door at home. Did this mean the one-armed bandits were clearing us out? Well, I guess they could've been. But what was I really focusing on? It was where the heck the next restroom was so I could relieve myself. That was about all I could focus on and the control I had at that time.

Who Was I Fighting With?

Out of nowhere, I would have full-out fights with my own mind! I was waiting for my coffee to finish dripping and I was playing out some argument that happened two days ago with someone I barely knew. I felt totally insulted and it stayed with me for literally two days.

Each drip I added to the story. My coffee was done, and I looked around and all I saw was my puppy Hope looking up at me, ready for belly rubs. That was it, it was the only thing happening. That person who pissed me off wasn't there, so who was I mumbling to? I laughed because I knew this person didn't give a rat's ass about how I was torturing myself. All I was doing was focusing on something that wasn't happening and started feeling angry! I barely remembered what I had for dinner the day before! As I grabbed my coffee, I gave my dog belly rubs. I focused on what was happening and it was really simple. Nothing besides me drinking my coffee and loving my puppy! This means that all the problems I experienced were nothing more than *thinking problems.*

Trash Talk

Reframing what I said to, **WAIT- W**hy **A**m **I T**alking, changed my world.

"Forget it, why bother trying, I'm going to hurt someone, I'm going to fail, I'm only a liability." The last statement was when I was sent to pretty much every area in the hospital, including the oncology, neurology, cardiology, and psychology units. A particular nurse wheeled me in as my weight plummeted as well as my strength and told me I was going to have someone sit with me. What? Was I that sick? Was there something they didn't tell me?

"Between your health and depression, you're our biggest liability." There it was another label I believed; I was just a liability. Again, I made it about the "mean nurse", but I had to look at my part. I was very sick. And, as sad as it sounds, I *was* a liability. This unsympathetic nurse could have used a better choice of words but that was out of my control. Why would any, decent, well-adjusted person speak to a terribly ill patient with such a lack of compassion or respect? I learned to let that go because it was about her and how she reacted.

Self-Talk

What do you secretly say to yourselves during a day, month, or lifetime? Some for me were: "I'm so sorry, I'm so stupid, I should have left earlier, I knew this was rush hour," I said as I flew in for my appointment with my life coach, and I hate being late!

She just smiled, as I was trying to tame my windblown mess of hair. Then I noticed a blob of my smoothie on my coat. I just smiled as if everything was going great. She saw through this.

"At least I remembered to bring that picture you asked me to." Even though I had no idea why, I just followed instructions. After our initial catch-up, she had a challenge for me.

It was to say, out loud, everything I secretly said to myself in my mind. That was easy! I didn't have to even think about it. "I'm such a mess, I'm sorry I was late and wasted your time, I'm a slob, I'm so stupid, and I hate my frizzy hair. All I wanted was to be a great mom, but I F#@%$! up pretty badly and lost it with my kids. I hate my stretch marks and I have no muscle. I'll never wear shorts. I'm such a burden."

She stopped me there. She put a chair right in front of me and put that picture she asked me to bring in from when I was a kid. She said, "Now say those things to that little girl." Even though I knew this was an exercise she did with many other people, it felt like I was the only one.

My eyes filled with tears, she was so sweet, had cute curls, and was so innocent. My throat swelled up, and I couldn't do it. That's when she reminded me that the little girl was me. So, if I wouldn't say it to her, why am I saying it to myself? I would never talk to my best friend this way. I needed to start being my own best friend.

We went through an exercise I call reframing. Instead of saying, "I'm sorry I'm late," (or sorry for anything), I would reframe it to, "Thanks for waiting."

"I'm sorry for bothering you," changed to, "Thanks for helping me out."

And yes, welcome to being a parent. We say and do things we don't mean, we're human too. Does it mean I'm a terrible mom? No! When we hear, "I hate you!" from our kids do they really hate us? No!

Wait For It!

I reframed how I spoke about my body. Do I look in the mirror and say, "Hey you sexy thing?" No, but I did see the beautiful way it could move, and how grateful I was to have the ability to be able to move at all!

Now, I stop myself and say WAIT. **W**hy **A**m **I T**alking to myself or out loud? I caught myself, sometimes after I already bullied myself, but the more I practiced, the more I was able to cut out the words shouldn't, can't, guilt, shame, burden, ugly, idiot, stupid, etc. The list was endless.

Reframing things practically saved my life. Your brain doesn't know if what you're telling it is true or not, it simply follows it. Little by little, reframing was instrumental in every part of my life. Instead of saying what I didn't want, I said what I wanted. "I don't want to be broke," became, "I want to have money."

"I don't want to feel depressed," became, "I want to feel good, even happy!"

"I dread exercising," became, "I want to get fit and strong to stay healthy." I became very mindful to state what I wanted.

I felt my face turn beat red, my muscles tense, and my eyes start to fill with tears. "I will never walk again; I'll be chained to my walker."

Here was my opportunity to destroy this negative self-talk. I took control and changed absolutely everything I could in a positive way. So, I said, "I *used to* hate to use my walker, *but now* I'm committed to doing my exercises and will walk again."

Skip The Pain, Experience The Pleasure

Just using the words **used to**, then, **but now** shows our brains that we're doing things differently. To keep the momentum, I added **because**. "When I *used to* need my walker, I hated it, **but now** I'm committed to doing my exercises **because** I can't wait to dance with my husband at our anniversary

Use this in any area you want to change. It creates the best motivation and works!

> "Whenever you say, 'I'm anything; you're commanding your mind and your body towards a destiny."
> DR. JOE DISPENZA

It was my secret weapon. I became aware of what I was thinking and told myself, **"I'm not my thoughts, I'm not my emotions."** I have the power to change my thoughts and my feelings!

Can you imagine what would happen if we actually behaved in the way that we talked to ourselves? In the past, I've said, "I'm going to die if I don't get an A or pass that test." "I'm going to be single forever because everyone I love leaves me." "I'm so stressed I'm going to pull my hair out!" Now guess what? I didn't die, I found love again, and I have hair!

Time to Bury Those Words!

I discovered four power words, and they are: I believe in you. The three power words are: I love you and I like you. Words that always hurt are I told you so.

It wasn't easy but slowly, my speech was coming back. That didn't stop me from trying to get my point across or my

Wait For It!

two cents in! I asked my husband for his feedback on how I talked. As he laughed, he said not much different than before! I was confused. He said, "Okay, let me give you an example."

Husband: Tells the story to the point in three minutes.

- Including key points only

Me: Telling the exact same story in 20 minutes.

- 25 insignificant details
- 11 back stories
- remembering I needed to add something to our grocery list.
- trying to get back on track by saying, "Where was I" about 7 times.
- 3 off-topic stories
- 4 times saying, "To make a long story short".
- maybe I'll finish later.

Well, that pretty much sums it up! Obviously, I had a lot of catching up to do! I now try to use WAIT: Why Am I Talking when I'm being mindful of our conversations. Remember I said I'll try!

For the Love of God, Stop the Complaining!

Remember it's not all about you. I was standing in line waiting for my night meds when I was really sick, and the nurse was huffing and puffing, complaining that not only did she work a double shift, but this was also her eighth day working in a row! She started complaining about how people take so long to take their medication. Well, I was one of those people who were so slow taking their medication. At first, I felt bad for her. I used to gag when taking more than one pill at a time. I would watch her look down the row at the other patients, so I quickly learned to take them all at once (well, mostly).

> "Be impeccable with your words. Speak with integrity. Say only what you mean. Avoid using the word to speak against yourself or to gossip about others. Use the power of your word in the direction of truth and love."
>
> DON MIGUEL RUIZ

Then, around 3 am, my pain flared up and I had medicine that was prescribed as needed for breakthrough pain. My normal medication was going to be given at 5 am, and I tried to get through it but had to push the button and ask for help.

"What is it, Christa? I'm busy with other patients and I haven't even had my break."

"Um nothing, I can wait." I sat in agony for two more hours because I didn't want to bother her. I mean she worked extra, and I already felt like a burden.

Wait For It!

People forget that their complaining can affect others, even when it's definitely not intentional. I want to state clearly that she was an amazing nurse, and yes, was working her butt off, but what was the benefit of telling us how shitty it was?

Take this example and put it in any scenario. No one wins and everyone suffers. The others who hear you complain will feel it and be affected by it, but you'll never know it. It really works when you start becoming aware of what you're saying. I had a full conversation with my mom, catching her up on my kids, and life in general. As we ended the conversation she said, "So it sounds like you're feeling good."

In reality, I forgot to tell her what really went on. I had a bad episode where I aspirated, and fluid filled my lungs. It felt like I was drowning. It wasn't an easy recovery, but I got through it. I also had two falls, but they were not serious. "Why didn't you tell me this?" she asked.

I totally forgot! I was aware that complaining about this illness only kept me feeling sorry for myself, and it became my identity. So, when people asked how I was doing, I didn't get into this drawn-out explanation about how many seizures or falls I had, or any other bad things that happened. I just said something like, "Today I'm having a good day," or, "Working on getting stronger" That's it. No need to draw it out.

Overall, complaining is simply a waste of time. Think of it, when you're with a group, what's the first thing you do? Complain about something. Then it feels like a competition, whose life is the shittiest, who worked the hardest, who had to deal with some alien who captured their teens or whose parents never understood them. Seriously, is it that you have slow internet, bad teachers, cranky co-workers, and a hangnail? And really, we all have bad moments but don't stack them up, so you create a bad life. We already went through that stuff, but complaining keeps you feeling like a victim and pulls the energy out of other people around you who have to listen!

Trust me, I get it. It's so easy to think some external force is out to get us. It's not as if God doesn't like you if it rains on your wedding day. It's just raining and sorry you can't plan that, but you can have a backup place to hold the event if the wedding is outside. If you stop your wedding because of rain, you probably didn't want to get married in the first place, so there's your excuse, blame it on the rain but don't complain!

Venting

After ruminating and probably making up some outrageous story over something small, I just had to vent to someone to get it off my chest, so they could give me advice, a different perspective, or tell me I'm an idiot, or whatever. It's still healthy. When it comes to those pent-up feelings, ignoring them is like trying to hide a burp in a crowded room—it will come out eventually and it's going to be awkward.

Now, on the other hand, gossiping is only spreading hate. One person shoots first, and then the other person, now wounded, tries to retaliate. Sounds like war, right? Well, it is. It can cause permanent wounds and possibly death.

Wait For It!

> "It takes a lifetime to build a good reputation, but you can lose it in a minute."
> — WILL ROGERS

So, how did you use your weapon? Being impeccable with your words and speaking with integrity? I interpret it in its simplest forms: use it for good not hate. Love not pain.

A Simple Plant

I can prove the true power of your words. You have the power to make a simple plant thrive and bloom or shrivel and die. Don't believe me?

The New York Post By Bradly Jolly

There was a study in a school that looked at the effects of bullying. Two plants had the exact same environmental conditions, soil, water, and sun but one plant had a speaker that played only praise and compliments and the other plant had a speaker playing nothing but insults.

The first plant was told: "Nobody likes you. No one notices you when you're in a room. You're a mistake. You look rotten. Why are you still alive?"

The second plant was told: "I like you the way you are. Seeing you blossom makes me happy. You're making a difference in the world. You're beautiful."

The results speak for themselves. The one that was beaten down with words shriveled and the one that received the praise grew and blossomed. If it can make a plant start to die, what does it do to your soul? This is a real picture of the plants in the experiment.

This quote says it all.

> "Your words control your life, your progress, your results, and even your mental and physical health. You cannot talk like a failure and expect to be successful."
> GERMANY KENT

We were at my daughter's basketball game, and the score was tied. I would say, "Look we're winning!" I mean, we weren't losing!

I had other moms say, "I'm sitting next to you because you're so positive."

It felt good to look through those lenses. Did we win? No, but I focused on how they were able to play the sport they loved, and how they made amazing friends. and as a bonus, the parents did too!

BE FREE AND STOP THE BS!

Belief Systems - BREAK THOSE CHAINS

I love this story I heard years ago. It's about a man who, as he was passing some elephants, suddenly stopped, confused by the fact that these huge creatures were being held by only a small rope tied to their front legs. No chains, no cages. It was obvious that the elephants could, at any time, break away from their bonds but for some reason, they did not.

He saw a trainer nearby and asked why these animals just stood there and made no attempt to get away. "Well," the trainer said, "When they are very young and much smaller, we use the same size rope to tie them, and, at that age, it's enough to hold them. They are conditioned to believe they cannot break away as they grow up. They believe the rope can still hold them, so they never try to break free."

> "Did you know that your brain will constantly rewire itself to suit the information that you feed into it? If you constantly complain, gossip, find excuses, etc; it will make it much easier to find things to be upset about, regardless of what is happening around you. Likewise, if you constantly search for opportunities, abundance, love, and things to be grateful for, it will make it much easier to find a reflection on those things around you. It takes practice, but over time, this is a very powerful way to reshape your reality."
> — GERMANY KENT

Again, if you believe you can't, you probably can't. Maybe from childhood, you were told you weren't good at something. It doesn't matter because whatever you believe is usually true and that makes you limit yourself. If you believe you aren't worthy or talented, it could be anything, and you'll stay stuck. The thought of failing would often hold me back from even trying. I've learned the best lessons in life from when I failed. I now knew what not to do! As upset as I was at

> "Life has no limits except the ones we create."
> — LES BROWN

Skip The Pain, Experience The Pleasure

> "You're not fat, you have fat. You also have fingernails, you're not fingernails."
> — UNKNOWN

the time, I couldn't see the bigger picture. I may have failed in one area, but an opportunity would show up that I would never have stumbled upon if I succeeded.

Once I realized this, it was like a new world opened to me, a world of opportunities and possibilities that would set me **FREE** from those heavy chains that kept holding me back in every area of my life.

To be **FREE** is all I wanted, and it worked. **F**ocus, **R**eframe, **E**vidence, and **E**liminate. These are not random words, it's a technique I used and shared with others to change the beliefs that held them back. Many of them came back in tears saying they never ever thought life could be so different. They developed newfound peace, excitement, and passion to go after the things they desired, including taking new risks. Instead of wasting time, the fears that held them back were gone! Let's get into it.

Focus on the specific beliefs you have that are holding you back. Take out that paper and pen. Don't overthink it, just do it! You'll know what they are when you simply ask yourself what you want, and then why you don't have it. Don't get tripped up, this is the time to let out all the kinks.

Reframe them and it will reprogram your unconscious beliefs. Ask yourself:

- What is my limiting belief? (Write down the belief that's holding you back from achieving your goals, desires, and dreams.)
- What would my life look like if I no longer had these limiting beliefs?
- Now choose what you want to believe instead. It's important to replace the old limiting belief with a new one.

Evidence: Look for evidence of when you were not what your boogie man was telling you. For example, "I'm an idiot." I bet you can think of hundreds of times you weren't throughout your life. And look at all areas of your life. Your *career* (working at home is a career too)/ *relationships/ health/ spirituality*, there are no limits. Don't rationalize this; it's not the time to create new BS!

Eliminate each limiting belief that you have. Eliminate all negative self-talk. It's a waste of time. Watch how you talk to yourself. Replace "I can't" with "I can", even if it feels totally foreign. Trust me, they're an illusion.

Some of *my* limiting beliefs were:

- I should stay quiet because of my lisp; I will sound like a fool when speaking.
- Why love when I'll lose it anyway? Who would want a single mom with extra grief?
- I'm an embarrassment so why try? I will fail and let others down.
- As a people pleaser, my boundaries were weak; I would rather people like me.
- I'm now disabled; I used to be able to do so much, and now I'm a burden.

Honestly, I still have those ugly beliefs that pop up but overall, I've tackled the biggies and am now free of any of these thoughts! After working through this process, I'm now able to:

- Do public speaking.
- Open my heart to love again, and be with someone who totally accepts me, my son, and my past.
- Appreciate the ability and confidence (sometimes with my service dog Hope) to go out and live life!
- I now have the freedom from those constant thoughts of "I can't" and I change them to "I can" or at least why the heck not try! I'll at least find out what didn't work. I leave all the excuses behind.

And let me tell you the best part about it is you don't have to wait for a crisis to change your life! You simply need to challenge the beliefs that are holding you back and you'll be free!

Stinking Thinking and a Negative Mind Will Never Grow Positive Results

Yes, stinking thinking is an unhelpful thinking style. *Did I miss this class in life?* I mean, I looked at these headings and they seemed too obvious, too easy. It wasn't until I shared them with others that I found out it was new to them too! When I looked at these thoughts, it was as if someone was reading my mind. Then I found out these were common for everyone. At least I knew I was normal! Well, some might say that's debatable! Let's take a whirl around my Unhelpful Thinking Styles.

Unhelpful Thinking Styles

All-or-nothing thinking: This thinking style is also known as "black-and-white thinking". It involves seeing things in extreme categories without any shades of grey. *"I either eat the entire cake or no cake at all. There's no in-between. Oh well, I guess I'll just have to eat the whole thing!"*

1. **Overgeneralization:** This thinking style involves making sweeping conclusions based on a single event. *"I failed one test in high school, which means I'll never succeed in life. Time to drop out and become a professional couch potato!"*

2. **Mental filter**: This thinking style involves only paying attention to the negative aspects of a situation and ignoring the positives. *"I got an A on my paper, but my teacher made one tiny comment about my grammar. I guess I'm a terrible writer and should just give up now."*

3. **Disqualifying the positive:** This thinking style involves rejecting positive experiences or accomplishments by thinking they don't count for some reason. *"Sure, I won the lottery, but it was only $15. What's the point? I'm still broke."*

4. **Jumping to conclusions:** This thinking style involves making assumptions about a situation without any evidence to support them. *"I saw my boss whispering to my co-worker, so they must be talking about how terrible of an employee I am. Time to start job hunting!"*

5. **Magnification and minimization:** This thinking style involves either exaggerating the importance of negative events or minimizing the importance of positive ones. *"I know I saved a cat from a tree, but that doesn't matter because I forgot to take out the trash this morning. I'm such a failure!"*

6. **Emotional reasoning:** This thinking style involves assuming that your emotions reflect reality. *"OMG! I borrowed my boyfriend's phone and just dropped it in the toilet! Crap, I'm a loser. I mean, what kind of idiot brings their phone to the bathroom anyways? I feel like sh*t!"*

7. **Should statements:** This thinking style involves imposing unrealistic expectations on yourself or others. *"I should be able to eat whatever I want without gaining weight. Why does my body have to be so unfair?"*

8. **Labelling and mislabelling:** This thinking style involves putting negative labels on yourself or others based on a single event or characteristic. *"I accidentally cut someone off in traffic, so I'm obviously a horrible person and should never be allowed to drive again."*

9. **Personalization:** This thinking style involves taking responsibility for events that are beyond your control. *"My friend canceled our plans, so it must be because they hate me and don't want to spend time with me. Time to go cry in a corner again!"*

Did these examples help?

I wanted to say this quote from Homer Simpson, *"Shut up brain, or I'll stab you with a Q-tip."* It was amazing how easily I was able to discover the number of times I ping-ponged between these unhelpful thinking styles that kept me up at night! This was one of the best tools I've learned about. I hope you find it useful.

Are we doomed to a life of holding those hurtful thoughts spinning on plates, making sure we don't drop one? No! Of course not! Here are some strategies that help.

FIRST: This may be too obvious but read each one and see if you can identify with them. For me, I can have two or three going on simultaneously! You can't learn them from osmosis (if you can, let me know how). If you've already seen this, use it as a refresher.

SECOND: Catch yourself doing it. How do you know if you're doing it? It's easy! You feel like crap! We all experience unhelpful thinking styles, and once we can identify how they're impacting our thoughts; we'll have the awareness to step back and strive to change those thoughts.

So, what are the steps I came up with to stop myself from going off track? I came up with an acronym for **STOP:**

- **S** - Stop - I would actually stop what I was doing.
- **T** - Thoughts - I would check out my thoughts and see if I was making things seem like a catastrophe or having some good old words that only made me more upset.

- **Opposite** - Opposite action - I mean however I wanted to react, I would turn around and do the opposite. Sometimes I had to give myself a time-out in my room, but at least I didn't react.
- **P** - Plan/Paced - These stands for two things. First, follow a plan. I was always being asked for money and had a hard time saying no. But I developed a plan and would ramble off the memorized lines and end the conversation. The second was paced breathing. Instead of holding my breath, I would pay attention to it and breathe in for the count of four, hold it, breathe out for the count of four, and repeat until I felt myself become more relaxed.

Find a Way Even Using a Cat Claw

I still fell into the traps in my head that kept convincing me that I can't do something. My mother and stepfather bought me a beautiful art piece of trees to hang on my wall. They knew I love trees and every time I look at it, it reminds me of my dream of planting 100,000 trees around the world. Yes, big dream. The nail came loose, and the picture dropped. My hands were achy and swollen; I could barely hold the nail straight, so I waited days until my husband would fix it. Time went on, and yes it was a picture, not my last meal, but it was bugging me. Deep down what was really bugging me was the fact that I couldn't do it myself.

Then I remembered we had this small hammer and pry bar thingamajiggy called a cat claw in a drawer. I grabbed it, and it was small enough for my hands to get around and had just enough grip so I could smash that nail in! Ok, I guess tap it

Wait For It!

but to me it felt like I smashed through that, "I can't ever do it because of my hands," to "I am hell-bent on finding some way to get this picture up!"

Every time I look at it, it reminds me that there's always a way unless I want to let excuses win!

Summary of Insights

- **Every decision you make, every choice, can change your life.**

- **The way you think and what you focus on becomes your reality.**

- **It isn't about making the best life; it's making the best life every day you live.**

- **Your words are your superpower; they can build or destroy you. Remember it can take a lifetime to make a reputation, but a moment to break it.**

- **WAIT-What Am I Thinking? Why Am I Talking?**

- **What you believe is true becomes true. You have the power to change your beliefs and change your life!**

- **STOP - When you need to change your thoughts and if you're about to react.**

Chapter 9

PLEASING MYSELF

Investing in your self-care is essential for self-love.

YOU HAVE TO TAKE CARE OF YOURSELF FIRST INSTEAD OF GIVING THE WORLD WHAT'S LEFT OVER.

Self-Care

When you're on a plane, they always say to put your oxygen mask on before helping anyone else. You can't help anyone if you can't breathe! You might have heard this before, but even though I've heard it a zillion times, I never really thought about what it had to do with self-care. I finally got it. You won't be able to help anyone else unless you take care of yourself first. I was happy with a daily shower, using a new razor, using a nice moisturizer once in a while, and sitting with my family to eat instead of standing and serving. Then I found out that isn't enough self-care at all. I found out it's unique for each person and I decided to go all in and made a list. Mindfulness, meditation, yoga, spending time in nature, and journaling worked best for me. There are many more, but I started with these. So here was my plan for my self-care day.

First, I made sure I had arranged my schedule so I would have total undivided attention for ME. I think that deserves a gold star! Now, mindfulness. I focused on my house plant, looking at the shape of the leaves and the way the stem bent. What is with all that dust? Oh, this is a fake plant, but you can practice mindfulness with anything. The petals were a beautiful white, well maybe yellowish because the sun faded them. Stop thinking about that. Now, back to being mindful. The vase has dimples that I didn't realize before and three dimples with dark gunk in them. Okay, I was done with that. I grabbed a cloth and quickly wiped down the plant but did not do a thorough cleaning because I was practicing self-care, not cleaning.

On to meditation. I sat on the soft carpet with my legs folded, arms opened, and back straightened. I pressed play on my app which was leading me through a guided meditation to promote being calm and relaxed. This is what I needed, and it was free so double bonus. It was beautiful, soft music—wait, too soft, I had to turn it up. A man's voice, sounding like he was trying to pick me up at a bar, instructed me to start with any tension in my neck and let it go. Let my arms go heavy and my legs and feet droop. Soften my jaw and take three slow, deep breaths. With one inhale, I coughed but that was ok. Should I pause it? No, keep it going.

Pleasing Myself

His seductive voice told me to clear my mind, and if thoughts come in, let them float by like clouds. Clouds, there were dark clouds, was it going to rain? I would need to bring in my cushions. Now, back to my meditation, I pressed the button, oh yeah, let go of thoughts, wait isn't that a thought? I'll focus on the music. But what do I do with the bit of snot that was going to run down my face? I mean, even monks have to blow their noses. I could only suck it up so many times, so I grabbed the closest Kleenex and blew whatever I had in me so I could finish my self-care meditation. I didn't pause it because I figured blowing my nose was self-care.

Now, onto yoga. I checked my gym's schedule, and it was full. I checked out another yoga studio and I missed the time. Oh well, I tried, so that counts. I decided since it wasn't raining, I would continue my self-care and walk barefoot in the grass. I enjoyed the softness, and the sound of the birds. Oh, crap, literally, who the heck left the dog's poop? I grabbed the pooper scooper and got rid of the evidence. Ahh, now I'm getting mad. Dang it, no! This is my self-care time, and I will take those three slow breaths and be happy. Great, I grabbed my coffee and journal and wrote the following, "My self-care day was amazing," and then crossed that out. "I feel at peace," no…I put a big red x over that. Well, I did it! Check!

I don't know much about self-care, but I don't think checking off a list of things you should do was the best idea. How do people do this stuff? Well, those people are not me. I had to figure out what self-care meant for me. I realized it was time alone without the need to clean, wash, cook, fix, or change a light bulb. Here's an example of one of myself-care days.

I started off by taking a nice, hot bubble bath. I got dressed and went for a small walk, just to the mailbox down the street but that was enough for me. I later went outside on my patio and walked in the grass while enjoying my hot cup of coffee. I laughed as I caught up with a friend on the phone while telling her about my accidental auto-correct incident! Later, I turned up the music, danced, or jiggled, while I sang my guilty pleasure song. At dinner, I grabbed some fresh lilacs from our bush and put them in the center of our table. Then I came into my office and spent some time writing this book. It isn't a journal, but you know what? This was the best self-care day I had!

Remember to do what works best for you because losing ourselves is our biggest casualty. People will come and go in life, but the person in the mirror will be there forever. So be good to yourself. I know I will try meditation, yoga, and all that stuff in my own time, but it will not be because I think I have to do it, it will be because I want to do it and I won't pressure myself to do it all in one day!

I'm wondering if you had to list 50 names of those you love, what number would you put *your* name next to?

Investing in Myself

I didn't think twice when I dropped my kids off at the mall, handed them $40, and left. I was taking a course and didn't buy the book that goes with it because I knew I could figure it out online, plus it was a waste of money. It was $15. The truth was I wanted that book, not just for the course but for me. And it was as if I saw my day play out like a movie. I had no problem handing over money to my kids but wouldn't spend anything on myself.

"Do you want something from the food court?" they called and asked.

"No," I replied. I mean I had some leftovers I could eat, so why waste the money? There it was again.

Of course, I would have loved to have something fresh, especially because it was really my money, but I felt guilty if I spent any on myself. I feel selfish because I really don't need anything but knowing I could buy them something that would make them happy, well that's my soft spot.

From all of the conditions throughout my childhood, I figured it was my job to make money. Maybe it's those quiet thoughts we've been told that become our mantra.

- "Money doesn't grow on trees!"
- "Another day, another dollar."
- "No rest for the weary."
- "No pain, no gain."
- "We've been doing it for generations, now it's your turn to make us proud!"
- "Do you know what it takes to put food on the table?"
- "Do you know how many light bulbs are on that light fixture taking up energy?"

What's the real value of money? Well, $100 to a person who lives on the street is worth more than it is to a billionaire. Now, take a $100 bill and give it to someone who needs that much to make rent. Take a $100 bill and write that information you've been anxiously waiting for on it because it was the only piece of paper you could find (I actually did this). Essentially, it's just that: paper, but the value we place on it can vary widely.

I'm not saying it's easy to challenge those beliefs. Even though it was hard at first, I signed up for a weekend retreat. It seemed like way too much money, and I didn't want to spend it because our dryer broke. Spending money on me was like getting blood out of a stone, but my loving husband insisted. I can tell you it was one of the best decisions I made. And guess what? I can't wait for the next one! In those 48 hours, I met the most incredible people that I would have never met if I hadn't invested in myself! It was a bonus gift from the universe!

We have 86,400 seconds or 1,440 minutes in a day. How do you spend it? Well, let's get dressed, get ready for the day (add extra time for brushing your teeth, hair, makeup, etc.), eat, drive, sleep, and figure out how many minutes are left. It's what we do within those 24 hours that makes the difference.

At the drop of a hat, I would run to pick up something, drive someone, take extra work, and help at all costs only to burn myself out. I found out I was not really helping them because I knew perfectly well, they could have done it themselves. It's my natural instinct to fix others' problems. I used to say, if they're good, I'm good and if they're bad, I'm worse. This is what a

> If you carry a person all the time through the tough parts, they will never learn to walk.

co-dependent relationship looks like. So, let others learn by fixing their own problems, this is when they learn the most. If they fail, they'll be stronger for doing the exercise of solving their own problems.

So, you can spend your time counting your "likes" on social media or creating more likes for yourself.

Live Every Day with a Fresh Start

Ahhh, finally, I woke up smiling, feeling happy and refreshed after a great night's sleep. Then all of a sudden, I remembered that stupid pinhead that threw a tizzy, drawing attention to us in the grocery store when I grabbed the last pack of toilet paper. I mean we were totally out, and our unmentionables needed to be cared for too!

As I stumbled into the washroom, that hanging roll (and of course, it was on backward) reminded me of his ridiculous outburst.

Right away I replayed it in my head. So how did that serve me? I mean I woke up happy and had toilet paper, why let that episode ruin my day when it was already over? If you focus on problems, it keeps you from focusing on solutions! Think about this.

Dr. Joe Dispenza inspired me with his messages. Did you know we have approximately 70,000 thoughts in a single day? And did you know 98% of those thoughts are repeats from yesterday? And 80% are negative! Damn, I never realized I thought so much. If I stayed thinking the same way, those same thoughts would lead to the same choices, that would cause the same behaviors, and voila, you end up feeling the same way! It's like *Groundhog Day*! So, don't worry, be happy. Yesterday is done; today has begun. You can choose to make it a good one! Oops, it wasn't supposed to sound the same, I hope it didn't make it lame.

Strive for Happiness, Even on a Rainy Day

Can you relate to having one of those days when nothing seems to go right? It might feel as if you've gotten up on the wrong side of the bed. Here's a flashback from one of my mornings before work. I went to the refrigerator around 3 am to grab a snack. I opened the door, squinting because of the blinding light, but couldn't find anything. I shut the door, grabbed a drink of water, and then opened the door. I guess believing some magic fairy suddenly whipped up a midnight snack. I was so exhausted I ended up waking up late because I slept through my alarm.

As I got dressed, I was bloated, so I grabbed my stretchy pants and then took a sip of my coffee. I bumped my hand on the door and spilled the coffee on my newly-ironed shirt (and I hate ironing). I grabbed the first top I could find to change into and noticed a small stain. It was better than the coffee spill! Now I had to wipe up the spilled coffee and realized I was late (I never am) and then couldn't find my keys! I found them dropped underneath a random shoe and while picking them

Pleasing Myself

up, I dropped my phone, only to shatter the screen. Then, I opened the door and, yes, you guessed it, it was raining.

How overwhelmed do you feel just reading this? On days like this, do you wish you could go back to bed and start over? If we only we could. But since we can't, maybe there are ways to change at least part of the day. So how do you raise your mood and find some happiness on those days when everything seems to be going wrong? Here are a few things that help me:

- This is my secret weapon. Be intentionally grateful! Size doesn't matter, you'll find trivial things that we take for granted. Start doing this consciously and your subconscious mind will notice more things, even if it's the air you breathe. Chew some gum, blow a bubble, and be grateful. Some wish they had enough air to blow, but they don't.
- I had to flip my mindset from feeling that the day had already gone down the gutter. Yes, the morning was crazy, but that was only 20 minutes of my day. So, for the rest of the day, be intentional about having a positive mindset. Again, you can start by chewing some gum!
- Move! Listen to upbeat music and have a little dance party. Don't make excuses that you're jingly, heck, Jell-O jiggles and everyone loves Jell-O!
- Turn the lights on! Think of us humans as solar panels. Suck up some vitamin D and it will lighten up your mood and turn you on!
- Dress to impress! Put something on that you feel fabulous in. It will perk up your spirits all day! It doesn't matter if you even leave the house, that's not the point.

- SMILE! Show those pearly whites or shady yellows, it's not the color; it's the muscles that raise your cheeks that will raise your mood!
- Watch something funny. It will give you some dopamine, and don't leave out the "amine" part!
- We've all heard the saying when life gives you a lemon, make lemonade, or if all else fails, take it with a grain of salt, and then maybe add a shot of tequila!
- Now this line is for you to list what brings you happiness and pleasure. Fill in the blank _____

Cranky When Criticized?

> "We don't stop playing because we get old. We get old because we stop playing"
> GEORGE SHAW

Do you get defensive when someone corrects you? Join the club. Especially when you haven't even asked for their opinion! But, since we're talking about not taking things personally, this is where we must follow through. I finally did and it paid off.

I was asked to speak to a group about some of my experiences, and at the end when I was walking out, most people said how much they enjoyed it, however, one person told me it was good, but I should work on the introduction. So instead of hitting him over the head with my speech, I puffed out my chest, trying to look professional and said, "Interesting you say that. How so?"

"It was too long, and your speech ended up being too short. I would have loved to hear more of the story because I could feel your passion." That was it! If I didn't ask how so, I would have left feeling resentful and let's be real, basically pissed!

I saw his perspective and thanked him. I reviewed it and saw that he was right. My intro dragged on and took away from the passion of my message. What great feedback! Now, I'll be more mindful next time. It's hard to see imperfections in ourselves, so having others' opinions, even though they may sting, can add value. Turn what sounds like criticism into feedback!

It's Never About You

> "Nothing others do is because of you. What others say and do is a projection of their own reality, their own dream. When you're immune to the opinions and actions of others, you won't be the victim of needless suffering."
>
> DON MIGUEL RUIZ

Even Mother Teresa had haters! Considering that, I have nothing to complain about. No one is spared from how other people see you and their opinions come through the filter of their judgment and perspective. I looked weak; at least, that's what I thought. I looked at other people dressed stylishly, running errands while juggling work. You see, I made up all these stories of how I thought other people saw me, and what other people expected of me. I wasted so much time worrying about what other people thought. It didn't occur to me to ask myself what I thought.

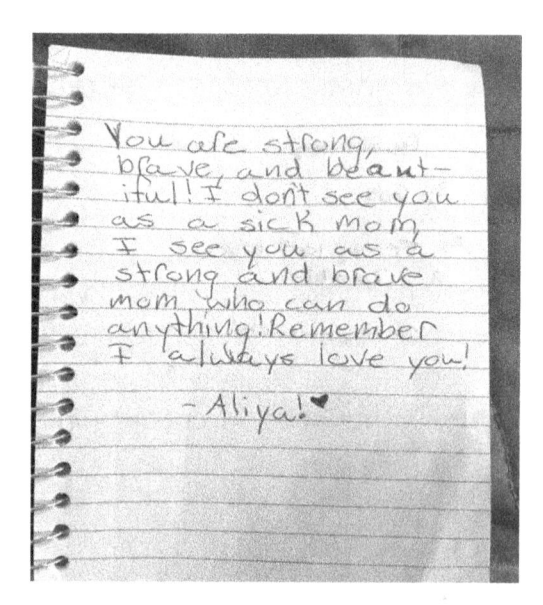

Here's a letter I randomly found in my notebook from my daughter. You see, I made up all these stories about how I couldn't be the mother I wanted to be, and all those memories from my car accident came flooding back. But wow, was I wrong.

> You are strong, brave, and beautiful! I don't see you as a sick mom. I see you as a strong and brave mom who can do anything! Remember I always love you!
> — Aliya! ♥

"It's not about you, don't take it personally. God, why are you so upset?" I would hear this a lot, but it was hard for me not to make it about me because of all those sneaky insecurities I had.

I would play out complete conspiracy theories. Why didn't someone accept my friend request on Facebook or follow me on Instagram? Why did my co-worker just brush me off and walk past me? It didn't really occur to me that they may have personal issues, pressures, or pain from hemorrhoids or diarrhea maybe? People come from all sorts of lives and backgrounds and maybe going through all kinds of problems. It's their own perception of their world that triggers their moods or past memories. It has nothing to do with you.

So, join the human race and realize it's not always about you. Everyone has their own sh!t they're dealing with, their own opinions, or maybe they're just self-centred, stuck-up jerks, but again, not your problem. It's not about you. I had to learn this lesson over and over, but I've got it now. Remember, all you can do is control how you think and feel, even if it's only empathetic.

Perfectionism - **Trying to Impress but Made a Mess.**

It was always such a big deal for me to make a good impression. My husband's uncle was coming down from out of town and it was the first time I was going to meet him. He was coming with my in-laws for dinner.

I planned everything down to a tee. I mean, I had the dinner music ready, homemade dressing for our salad, and of course, I wanted to start the dinner with perfect appetizers. That was one thing I rarely did. I talked to some people at work, and one was excited to tell me about these amazing jalapeno poppers. They were stuffed with a mix of cheese and not too hard to make. Perfect.

Following the recipe she jotted down on paper, I neatly arranged them on a platter; they were picture-perfect, Instagram-worthy. With new aesthetic napkins (does anyone remember what napkins they use?); I proudly passed the platter around as I seasoned the meat.

My mother-in-law took a bite and smiled; I knew it was a hit! Cue the music. One by one everyone grabbed one when finally, my mother-in-law said, "OMG these are burning my mouth! Do you have some milk and bread?" The others followed suit as they spit the remainder of my perfect poppers out.

I wanted to cry. I mean this was the first thing everyone tried, and I couldn't understand what went wrong! My husband pulled me aside and asked me if I made sure all the seeds were out. Whoops! That wasn't on the paper, and I guess common sense for me wasn't so common.

After trying to save the rest of the dinner experience, I fessed up and apologized for leaving the seeds in. So, our appetizers ended up being milk and bread! Everyone was trying to keep a straight face, but my husband giggled a bit, and then the rest of the table joined in on the laughter. The funny part wasn't how much they were in agony, it was how no one wanted to say anything!

At the end of the night, we hugged, and everyone had a great time. Did their incinerated mouths ruin the evening? Nope, nada, zilch.

After I left the pile of dishes, instead of worrying about cleaning up, I grabbed a glass of wine and looked around. It was definitely my real-life picture-perfect life!

I learned that even though I felt jealous when looking at all these beautiful families having dinner, I decided not to post my picture of my masterpiece. Instead, my hot mess ended up being one of the best memories that I could never have perfectly planned.

SAY YES!

It was easy to isolate myself, and the more I did this, the more I felt alone. I would complain about having no friends, yet I really didn't make any effort to see them. So, I made a deal with my hubby who was tired of me whining. The deal was that I would say YES to anything friends invited me to. Well,

Pleasing Myself

I ended up eating my words. I was asked to go out with my friend Jen to a karaoke place, just to relax and do something different. "As long as I don't have to sing!" I said.

My first go-to was to check with my husband, making sure we didn't have any plans (secretly wishing we did so I had an excuse). Nope, the night was free. I had to fight all the resistance but remembered my promise (and my hubby quickly reminded me as well), so I went and walked in looking for Jen. I didn't see her, so I sat at a table, grabbed a drink, and awkwardly flipped through the songs while trying not to make eye contact.

"Christa, is that you?" Cathy, an old school friend, asked. "I wouldn't have recognized you," she continued.

I wasn't sure if I should have been pissed, or if it was a compliment. "I'm here to meet my friend, Jen," I told her, hoping she would go away.

Nope, she grabbed a chair from the next table and rambled on about songs we used to sing at our sleepovers. I ran to the lady's room to call Jen. I sounded desperate when I was leaving a message on her voicemail. "Where the heck is she?" I mumbled, checking my messages.

As I walked out, all I heard was, "Ladies and gentlemen, please welcome Christa and Cathy doing a duet to *Manic Monday* by The Bangles."

Cathy dragged me up the stairs that were conveniently right next to the washroom. Probably because so many people threw up, I thought.

Skip The Pain, Experience The Pleasure

"NO!" I said. "I can't, I think I'm sick, I..." and the song began as Cathy shoved a microphone down my throat. Well, it felt that way.

I was sweating more than I would in a sauna! She stopped singing, cueing me to take over. Well, I didn't want to bring any more humiliation, so I followed the prompts and sang as low as I could. It didn't matter because the DJ just turned the microphone up. I looked around and felt relieved most people were just chatting and eating and then I saw Jen come in!

"Whoop Whoop! That's my friend Christa on stage she yelled."

Yes, all eyes went on me. I could have fainted, but I looked at Cathy smiling and having a great time, and that made me laugh. What the hell, "It's just another manic Monday," we belted out together.

She was laughing so hard, she said, "I think I peed myself a little."

Well, I started laughing so hard the more she laughed! I got off stage, and Jen apologized for being late. I wanted to throttle her, but I was too busy laughing!

Lying back in bed that night, I was still giggling, and as much as I wanted to say it was horrible, I found out it was fun. I had a great time and reminded myself to keep saying yes. I made new connections and became closer to friends, but no, didn't do karaoke again. Been there, done that, didn't need the T-shirt.

Take a Chance and Dink

Pickle? Paddle? Oh, Pickleball! My friend came for a visit and after hearing the joy in his voice talking about the sport, I decided to watch him. Of course, I wanted to look like I fit in, so I wore my sportiest clothes and watched with awe as he moved around, hitting the ball with ease.

"Ok, paddle up!" a very sweet lady said to me.

"Oh no, I'm just watching."

"Nah, come dink with me," she said.

Well, my mind went all over the place; I had no idea what she was talking about but I figured what the heck, and grabbed the paddle. I found out it was standing close to the net, lightly hitting the ball over. My friend looked over in shock, knowing I had limitations, but I was on the court!

Well, I was hooked. I started to dink around a bit more, then practiced some serves, trying to wrap my mind around the rules. "What's the score?" should be written on my T-shirt!

Did I have to rest after and find ways to deal with the pain? Yes, but I didn't let it stop me from going out, doing the best I could and meeting some pretty incredible people along the way, even if it meant I just showed up and found someone to dink with!

Summary of Insights

- **Self-care is individualized. Stay open-minded but ultimately, there's no checklist. Invest in yourself, you're worth it too.**

- **Start each day with a fresh start! Time is too valuable.**

- **Don't take things personally. People have a right to feel the way they do but I can choose to agree with them or not.**

- **There's no such thing as perfect. It's like chasing a unicorn.**

- **Say yes and get out of your comfort zone. Connect with friends because life is too short to avoid a chance to have fun. The bonus is you become better friends, and that alone is worth it.**

- **There is no such thing as limitations to taking a risk. Yes, it may not be in every situation but there is always a way to be part of it as long as you are willing to take a risk.**

Chapter 10

F@!&%^! IS YOUR ANSWER

Forgiveness is the key to freedom.

It's the F word. You know, "forgive". You can choose to forgive or hold a grudge. We all have free will! It's one of the hardest things to do. One thing that you must consider is every time you don't forgive, you re-traumatize yourself! That's right, you're the one who keeps that memory alive, and it continues to hurt you, not them. Trust me, you'll find out how much lighter you'll feel.

Keeping resentment is like drinking poison and wishing the other person would die. All you're doing is killing yourself

Skip The Pain, Experience The Pleasure

inside. I remember leaving home so upset that I had a wrestling match in my brain. Should I go get a doughnut or smash the windows of their car? The doughnut tasted good but for a split second, all I wanted was revenge. Forgiveness doesn't mean the damage didn't exist. It simply means the damage no longer controls your life.

Oprah Winfrey seemed to explain it best for my mind to wrap around it: **"I stopped giving up hope that the past could ever be different."** I realized only my perspective can.

Let that sink in. It finally hit me like an epiphany that it doesn't excuse what others have done or make it okay. It's forgiving that it was THEIR beliefs, choices, and actions, not mine. It's cutting the chain to the past, allowing you to move forward. Trust me, they're still left with their chain but that's no longer attached to you. This is the key to having inner peace. Forgiveness is not about letting go of the past, it's about freeing yourself from the pain it holds over you.

View your *tormentors* as *mentors*. Ask yourself, "What is this person meant to teach me?" Every person in our lives has a lesson to teach. Some lessons include: how to be stronger, how to use your voice, when to trust your gut, how to be more self-loving, when to let go, and why you want to be nothing like this person! When you say sorry, mean it. When you mean it, change it. When someone says sorry to you, accept it, because you'll be in the same position eventually. Don't hold grudges.

Also, don't forget to forgive yourself! This is the best gift we give ourselves. We're all human and anchored by our emotions. Make amends whenever possible, learn the lesson, and change your actions moving forward. I'll be the first to admit it, I screwed up big time! I can change the sign I kept wearing that said "kick-me" to a "kick-ass" sign!

> "Your past mistakes are only meant to guide you, not to define you."
> ZIAD K. ABDELNOUR

Don't Say Yes When You Mean No!

SETTING BOUNDARIES

The Cambridge Dictionary defines boundaries as, "A real or imagined line that marks the edge or limit of something."

It sounds easy enough when you're putting up a fence, but how about personal boundaries? Boundaries are different between humans. You're unique and you must set the boundaries that are right for you. An example for me was when I went for an interview at an old deli. I was young and wanted to make a good impression, so I wore a skirt and a nice top. The interview started off as normal, but then I felt the questions became odd, and I started to feel uncomfortable.

One of the last remarks the guy made was that if I wore a shorter skirt it would have made the interview easier. I was shocked because I'd never been talked to like that before, especially by an adult! I was confused but still accepted the job. I should have listened to my instincts because he ended up being totally inappropriate, and I quit. I left feeling sick, and I thought this guy seemed creepy. My instincts were right because years later, I found out in the news that he had several charges against him.

Never ever go against your gut. When it tells you something isn't right, follow it, or at least talk to someone about it. Boundaries are sacred and when something gets close to the line, that's the time to speak up. Make it clear that you're not going to change your decision, whatever the situation is. "NO" is a complete sentence.

Boundaries can be changed at different times and in different situations.

One of the biggest problems for me was how to say no because I was so afraid of hurting someone's feelings. I've talked to many people about this. This is a growing problem because many people are overworked, over-scheduled, and over-committed. I was looking for validation so much that I would do extra work, hoping to have any type of positive feedback. It wasn't until I was nearly burned out that I started creating boundaries in all areas of my life.

Here are some ways to say "No":

*No. But thanks for reaching out.

*I wish I could, but I have other commitments I've already made.

*I'm a bit overloaded right now.

*And don't forget you can simply say no!

Goals, Go Get Them! Work Smarter, Not Harder!

SMART goals are a clever way to set objectives that are specific, measurable, achievable, relevant, and time-bound. Let me break it down:

> "A long time ago people who sacrificed their sleep, family, food, laughter, and other joys of life were called saints. But now, they are called professionals."
> — UNKNOWN

- **Specific:** Your goal should be clear and well-defined. Don't be vague like trying to, "write a book someday." Instead, be specific like, "I will write 7 steps on how to train a goat to mow your lawn and fertilize it too!"
- **Measurable:** You need a way to track your progress. For example, set a target like, "I will write 500 words, four days a week because the other 3 days I'm training a goat."
- **Achievable:** Be realistic about what you can accomplish. Trying to write a 1000-page epic in a week might be a tad unrealistic (and if you can, tell me the secret!)
- **Relevant:** Your goal should matter to you and align with your interests. Writing a book about tie-dye basket weaving probably isn't your passion.
- **Time-bound:** Set a deadline to keep you motivated. "I will finish my book by the end of September so I can have my great book reveal while showing off my perfect lawn!"

Skip The Pain, Experience The Pleasure

> "The truth is that we can learn to condition our minds, bodies, and emotions to link pain or pleasure to whatever we choose. By changing what we link pain and pleasure to, we will instantly change our behaviors."
> — TONY ROBBINS

Make your goals **positive**; focus on what you want to achieve, instead of what you'd like to lose or not have. You should also think about what it is that you really want. For example, you don't want to *buy your dream car*, you want to *drive in it*.

Am I Moving Toward My Dreams?

I suggest you write out your to-do list. How much of it is close to your dreams? Let me give you an example.

Five of my goals are:

1. Walk a 5K.
2. Write a book.
3. Travel to a resort with my family.
4. Stand under a waterfall.
5. Plant 100,000 trees around the world.

And what are five things I did today?
How do these goals align with what I did today?

1. Walk a 5K – I loaded the dishwasher (I could have gone for a walk, using a cane or not, to build up endurance while the dishwasher was running).
2. Write a book – Well, I checked e-mails and scrolled aimlessly through social media.

3. Travel to a resort with my family – Folded the never-ending laundry instead of researching places to go.
4. Stand under a waterfall – Washed more dishes.
5. Plant 100,000 trees around the world – Helped pick some weeds.

How many of those things brought me closer to my dreams? None. Yeah, I don't see it either.

Every moment my emotions started to feel down, I concentrated hard to see how I could add even a thread of something positive. I would act silly if I could, anything to bring happiness became my motivation. I had to remind myself that I made a decision to get better, especially after all my falls, even if I was banged up and bruised, that I got up!

Accept responsibility for your actions. Be accountable for your results. Take ownership of your health

There is this acronym, **HALT**: **H**ungry, **A**ngry **L**onely **T**ired.

It was like the mother from down under would erupt, and she was ugly, well, at least I felt that way. I went shopping with my kids, and totally pushed myself to keep going because I didn't want to "waste time". My endurance sucks. The next day I could only push it for maybe five minutes, and I was done. I would also go hours without eating and let me tell you, I've never made a good decision when being hangry (hungry and angry), just ask my family. We're all different, but our bodies all need to have our basic needs met. Remember to ask yourself to HALT when feeling stuck in the mud. Ask yourself what you need to do to satisfy it, and instead of getting stuck in the mud, pull someone in and start mud wrestling. Or just grab a sandwich and go back to bed, your choice!

Am I aligning my behaviors with my values? If I value wellness, am I making choices that empower my mind, body, and soul? If I value my relationship, do I focus on the one or two things that the other person did wrong or do I praise them for the numerous things they do for me, most importantly for accepting me fully the way I am?

What actions am I doing to improve all my relationships? Am I a good friend? If I value joy, how am I showing up in this world? Do I consciously find ways to bring happiness to the world, see opportunities to have fun, and make someone's day instead of complaining or being selfish? If I value love, do I let fear stop me from following my passion? Do I criticize or build people up? Do I judge or love unconditionally?

I let my values be my GPS in life. Keeping these values as my north star keeps me returning to the same path.

Self-Sabotage and Perfectionism

This is my fifth year writing this book! Why is this so hard? It's probably because I'm not supposed to write a book and every time someone would come into my life and say, "You need to write a book!" I start and stop. Guess why? Because it was never perfect. I wouldn't even try unless I knew it would work out. Seriously, my inner perfectionist would repeat, "I have to have everything in my life organized and perfect so that when I do die, no one will criticize me!" Guess what? I failed, I'm alive and my socks aren't all matched—some even have holes! And I'm working on this book. Done is better than perfect!

I Will Do It Later

When is it later? Maybe tomorrow, next weekend when the kids get older, or when I get more sleep! You know what? I need to make a coffee, and I'll tell you tomorrow.

What motivated me? Someone told me the truth. They asked me what the purpose of writing this book was and I said, "I want to inspire others who are dealing with any sort of pain, find hope by sharing what I learned from some of my experiences."

Then they dropped this: "Well, how many people are you going to help if you don't finish this book?" Don't you hate those people who are right? So here I am, finishing this book.

Summary of Insights

- **Forgiveness is the best gift you can give to yourself. You'll take back your power and feel free of resentment.**

- **Boundaries are individualized. Stick to them. NO is a complete sentence.**

- **What steps are you making today to get closer to your dreams? Do you know what you want, what you really, really want? If not, that's fine. Start with what brings you happiness and work towards the steps to get you there.**

- **Be SMART with your goals. Self-sabotage is only an excuse to keep you stuck. If you keep doing the same things over and over, the things you do won't change.**

- **HALT! Hungry, Angry, Lonely, Tired? Check in with yourself and fulfil your needs.**

Chapter 11

CLIMAX OF LIFE

You have a purpose just because you were born.

You have a purpose just being born. No one is given a set path and thank goodness! You'll go through new experiences that will teach you valuable life lessons. The best part of living your purpose is that most of the time, you have no idea that you're fulfilling your purpose! You might crawl into bed, thinking about your day, but you don't know how it impacted another person's day! Think about that. Something you did, somewhere you were, something you said, even if another person overheard it. It might have been a moment that changed their direction in life!

The book, *How Good Do You Want To Feel?* by Edward Michael Raymond, shares the story of two construction workers.

Skip The Pain, Experience The Pleasure

> "When you stay on purpose and refuse to be discouraged by fear, you align with the infinite self, in which all possibilities exist."
> — WAYNE DYER

Two workers building a bridge both asked the same question. What are you doing?

Worker 1 answers: I'm welding steel together to make this bridge (Correct answer).

Worker 2 answers: I'm working on this bridge that will connect two nations and transport millions of people to see each other's great countries (Correct answer).

Are you a bricklayer or building a cathedral? Are you plucking a string on an instrument or part of a symphony? Are you making sandwiches for lunch or feeding a family? Are you just selling something or are you an integral part of a dynamic sales force that creates products to better our lives, and employs hundreds of people around the world who all benefit from it?

Are you still wondering what your purpose in life is? What if I told you that you fulfilled it when you stopped traffic for a dog that darted into the street? It was when you let the elderly couple take your parking spot that's closest to the door. When you act out of kindness, compassion, and love every day, in every possible moment, you're fulfilling your purpose.

> "The two most important days in life are the days you're born and the day you discover the reason why."
> — MARK TWAIN

Climax of life

Life for me continued to be a battle, and I remember grabbing my coffee, sitting on our back deck, and watching the sun begin to set. I felt no beauty. I felt no happiness. I felt almost useless, even though I made it through so much didn't mean I didn't still struggle. I didn't feel like it but my husband reminded me I hadn't been out of the house for a couple of weeks so we should take the dog to the dog park. I tried to think of a reason not to go, but since it was about my dog, I went. Heck, I already lived through karaoke, so I really didn't have an excuse.

We got there and walked around a bit and then I turned around and saw this beautiful lady, a friend we knew who beat cancer but then had a reoccurrence. I sat with her, and my husband continued the walk with the dog. I opened up about some of the ways I coped with the things I struggled with and there was no BS, pure honesty. "OMG me too!" she said as I could tell she could relate.

It was relieving for both of us to be able to talk openly, be authentic, and be courageous enough to tell the truth. It was as if we were the only ones there, the rest of the world shut out. After a long

> "You may think that you're completely insignificant in this world. But someone drinks coffee from the favorite cup that you gave them. Some heard a song on the radio that reminded them of you. Someone read the book you recommended and plunged headfirst into it. Someone smiled after a hard day's work because they remembered the joke that you told them about today. Someone loves themselves a little bit more because you complimented them. Never think that you have no influence whatsoever. Your trace, which you leave behind with every good deed, cannot be erased."
>
> UNKNOWN

hug, I went back to the car and saw the orange horizon from the sunset. It was beautiful, and I felt happy. She sent me a text saying how much I inspired her. She was thankful for my raw honesty, and she said she now found hope. I knew I was put there for a reason; my purpose for the day was to be part of her life.

Your Biggest Battle Might Be Your Blessing in Disguise

What Doesn't Kill You Makes You Stronger
What? I can think of many other ways I would love to have blessings. I mean I thought I had a handle on life until it broke. In my experience, my greatest tragedies were my greatest gifts. You see, this is how I learned the lessons of life. I know there's more to learn but I now come prepared with a few more tools. The blessings are that I can identify with others because I've been there. I can reach down into the deepest layers of my being and pull out the pain, suffering, fear, and utter chaos, and share the steps I took to keep going. These experiences have given me my soul's purpose which is to hold hope for others. I've been told that my journey may be the roadmap that could help someone else.

My childhood made me mature far beyond my years. Surviving my car accident forced me to hit a bottom that allowed me to get the help I needed to deal with my husband's death. As I held him in my arms, I experienced a life-changing moment of the deepest love you could ever imagine, as he passed from this world to the next. Through our marriage, I discovered what true love and commitment were, and I was able to remarry knowing it was possible. The blessings of my kids gave me the

Climax of life

experience of living my life differently, because of the amazing people they're growing into. The blessing of my illness showed me that through pain, you can learn to be resilient. Your ego says, "Once everything falls into place, I will find peace." Spirit says, "Find peace and everything will fall into place."

I questioned why I had to go through so much. That was until one day, when I was feeling down on the anniversary of Rob's death, and my little girl grabbed my hand and said, **"I'm sorry your husband died, but if he didn't, you wouldn't be my mommy."** Need I say more?

There should be a sequel to the number of times miracles like this happen. The universe is listening. When you want something, the universe has a beautiful way of helping guide you to where you need to go, what you need to do, and how to take the next step. Have you had a crazy dream or did someone pop into your mind? Then you get up and the phone rings and guess what? It was that person. Often, it turned out to be the answer I was looking for.

I continued to check it out and it ended up taking me on a journey that was not what I was expecting but better for myself or someone I was helping. The more I noticed this happening, the more it happened! It was as if there were two paths, one would be lighter, and I would instinctively know to follow it. Try following your intuition. Pay attention to when you feel led or give or receive information that just so happened to be exactly when you needed it, or when someone else did.

My husband often liked joking after a golf game, "For me, if I hit it right, it's a slice, if I hit it left, it's a hook and if I hit it straight, it's a miracle."

Miracles—My Angel at Our Rest Stop

One example was when I was traveling home from a health test about two hours away. We stopped at a rest stop to take a break. We got food and then I started shaking and slowly began having a seizure episode. I saw this lady who kept glancing at me. I was trying to cover up my shaking and I was feeling self-conscious, I mean did she have to stare?! I went to the bathroom and tried to put some water on my face. Out of the blue, she was standing next to me!

"You're not okay, it looks like you might be having a seizure, and you need to get out of the bathroom."

She told the kids they should check out the small gift and snack shop to give me some space to recover. My husband was able to get my meds. It turned out she was a recently retired nurse. She stayed with me, making sure I was safe until I was able to come out of it. She saw my exhaustion and asked if we wanted to spend the night at her house, as the weather was bad, and I might need more help. WHAT? Someone invites some strangers into their house, and what are the chances that a nurse was at the same rest stop, at that exact moment (and thankfully followed me into the bathroom)?

I teared up as I thanked her, only realizing after that going to the washroom alone was not a good idea. We thanked her for her help and compassionate offer, but we were close to home and a hospital if things got worse. She was my angel at the rest stop. As I write this, I pray she reads this and knows without a doubt how special she is.

Climax of life

I've asked the angels for help with anything from losing my diamond ring or losing a key. When I lose something, I say a prayer I learned as a young child. "Dear St. Anthony, please come around, I've lost my (item) and it cannot be found. Please help me find it." In one way or another, it shows up, and I'm very thankful. So, there is no limit to asking! Maybe you want to call it good timing, luck, even just a coincidence, or maybe synchronicity. Or it just could have been a miracle.

I had a hard time with the word "God". Each night we would have to kneel down and pray to God that our souls wouldn't burn in the fiery blazes of hell. All throughout life, it felt like anything bad happened, it was as if I was being punished. One night, I was suffering and knew there was a power greater than my own. I had to develop my own relationship with the God of my understanding. I don't care if you call it your higher power, consciousness, creator, the name doesn't matter. This God is a forgiving, loving God, not the punishing one that I grew up with.

I would have a conversation with God, which some may call praying. It's how you choose to live your life by using your words, beliefs, and actions. I believe we all have it within us, as they refer to the great "I am". If you feel the need to go into a building, a church, or whatever. If it's right for you, then do it. But worshiping in a building on Sunday and not acting along the lines of your faith in everyday life doesn't work. Just because you sit in a church doesn't automatically make you a Christian, any more than standing in a garage makes you a car. Ultimately, I can only speak for myself, but the God of my understanding has no limits, no judgment, and puts people and opportunities in my path and it's up to me to take advantage of it.

INTUITION

Your intuition comes from your higher self, your God within, or simply your gut feelings. It's when you feel inspired. Inspired means **in spirit.** It's saying slowdown, there's a crash about to happen. It's that thought of buying that certain gift, having an inner knowing that it's for a reason, and then the reason appears.

> "I don't think that anything happens by coincidence... No one is here by accident... Everyone who crosses our path has a message for us. Otherwise, they would have taken another path, or left earlier or later. The fact that these people are here means that they are here for some reason."
> — JAMES REDFIELD

Once you realize that you're a spiritual being having a human experience, you have the power to change and create extraordinary results in your life. You're more powerful than any situation you face! You're the one that creates the results in your life. Life is not happening to you; life is happening through you.

Intuition is like a sneaky ninja that hides in the shadows of your mind, ready to jump out and surprise you with insights and ideas that you didn't even know you had. It's like your brain's secret weapon, always there to help you make quick decisions and navigate through life's tricky situations.

Think of it like a sixth sense, a gut feeling, or a little voice in your head that whispers, "Hey, trust me on this one." Sometimes intuition is so subtle that you might not even realize you're using it, but other times, it's like a slap in the face making you say, "Wow, I can't believe I didn't think of that before!"

Climax of life

If you're deciding between buying a red or grey car, you flip a coin. Heads is red and tails is grey. If it's heads and you feel excited, that's your intuition telling you what you desire. If it's tails, and it's grey, and you think ok, but feel disappointed, again, that's your intuition telling you, you wanted red so go for how you feel and honor it. The more you do and practice this, the easier it becomes to sense it.

So, there I was, attempting to do yoga with a broken toe, feeling sorry for myself. Then I had a quick flashback of all the hurdles I had to jump through and thought, *if this is my biggest problem, I'll take it!* As I was leaving, I overheard talk about rare diseases. My gut dragged me back in against my will. I interrupted and shared my experience with my disease called Anti-GAD 65. I went from seizures to attempting to do yoga (which actually didn't go as well as I hoped but at least I tried!).

Turns out, the person had a personal story about her son's mysterious symptoms. We both ended up in tears, sharing our struggles. She confessed she was on the verge of a breakdown. I told her I'd been there too and started sharing my journey.

We both needed to hear each other's message. I told her I was writing a book and she said to hurry up and write it because she needed it! If I hadn't followed my gut (when I was uncomfortable) and taken a chance to tell her about my illness and how I found hope (like the **H**eck **O**ver **P**leasing **E**veryone and **H**old **o**n **P**ain **E**nds), we both would've missed an opportunity that inspired me to keep going, even with a broken toe.

Skip The Pain, Experience The Pleasure

My son was about 16 and told me he was going to ride his bike to meet his friends at a park. When he told me this, my stomach sank. There wasn't a real reason; he was old enough and rode his bike hundreds of times. This time, something was different, a fearful feeling washed over me. So, for some reason, I asked a million questions that there was no need for, but it was as if I needed to stall him. Finally, he just said, "So can I go?" I had no logical reason to say no and tried my best to shake that gut feeling and just said yes. I'm wondering if you've ever had this feeling, either good or bad.

Even though this nagging feeling persisted, I kept myself busy. A couple of hours later, the phone rang. I immediately knew it was something about my son. How did I know? I have no idea, but it was my gut telling me. I answered, and it was my husband. The first thing out of his mouth was, "So he's going to be ok, but..." I could have told the rest of the story (well maybe not all the details) myself. He had an accident and was knocked out and a friend called an ambulance. My husband rushed to the scene. He was taken to the hospital, and yes, he was okay. He had a concussion, some major road rash, and bruises but was ultimately okay.

Note to self: "I told you so, sincerely, your intuition."

So, in a way, intuition is like your brain's BFF, always looking out for you, ready to offer guidance and support when you need it most. And let's be real, we could all use a little more ninja-like intuition in our lives!

I have learned that we all have gifts, and I've strengthened mine through the gift of intuition. I have found several ways to give direction and clarity to others as well as myself in so many areas of our lives. I have been open to connecting to the spirit world, and the more I allow and explore these areas, the stronger they get.

As I continue to strengthen my gift for connecting with my intuition, I am always amazed at the outcome, especially when helping others. It's like finding the key that opens the lock to a whole new set of possibilities.

The Big Mani-*fast*ation (so damn quick!)

I was sitting back in my chair, waiting for my coffee, while I looked outside the window, watching others go about their lives. I was stuck in a rut and didn't know how to get out of it. I asked myself, what is it that I really want? Instantly, freedom and happiness came up. What brings me happiness is when our whole family can get together, but we only had a small car that didn't have enough seats for everyone.

I was browsing through my phone and a picture of a blue Ford Explorer seemed to illuminate off the screen! I instantly thought of taking my whole family to one of my favorite places, a beautiful greenhouse, and going on a small vacation to this beautiful gorge. I instantly felt free and happy just having the thought. I took a screenshot and sent it to my husband and said we're going to have this in three months, and then said, no, three weeks! Don't ask what came over me, but I knew I was on the right path. A few days later, my husband and I had an appointment at the bank.

Now to give you some context, between his work, life, and the kids' sports, we barely got to see each other. We had about an

Skip The Pain, Experience The Pleasure

hour until our next appointment, and he suggested we drive around to some dealerships. We saw the Ford dealership, looked at some used ones, and as we turned the corner, there it was! The same blue SUV that I screenshot. Both of us were in shock. It was the only one. We went into the store and my husband's friend happened to be there that day, and I shared this story. The finances ended up working out, and we were all able to be together in the same vehicle to have some amazing adventures. This all happened because I had the true desire to find freedom and happiness and let go of how I was going to get it. It turned out better than I could've even imagined.

Summary of Insights

- **You have a purpose just being born.**

- **You never know whose life you changed at the end of the day.**

- **Our biggest battles are our biggest blessings.**

- **Miracles happen every day, every moment without you realizing it. Sometimes you're someone's miracle.**

- **We can all tap into our intuition; it can lead us down wonderful paths with joyful moments and sometimes enlightenment.**

- **Feel what you want, and the universe will bring it to you. This is manifestation.**

Chapter 12

DON'T LET OTHERS HOLD THE PEN

Write your story with no regrets at the end.

Skip The Pain, Experience The Pleasure

I wrote a letter to my younger self.

Dear Younger Me,

First, I owe you an apology for putting up with what you didn't deserve. You're amazing, resilient, and a survivor. You just don't know it yet. You see, I know the pain, fear, guilt, and shame you carry but none of that's real, it's like a mirage. I promise you, as time goes on, you'll fight through it, or even crawl through every obstacle, but you'll make it to the other side. I remember praying for a miracle to happen, but I had no idea at the time when it didn't happen that it was the real miracle.

Embrace your uniqueness and know everyone has insecurities; you don't have to hide yours. Secrets made you sick, angry, and most of all, bitter, even though you kept them in, so don't. You'll learn coping skills during life, but you have to live them first. I know you so well that you don't have to save the world, save anyone in it, raise the love frequency and God knows what else.

Don't hold all that responsibility. Join in on some amazing adventures. While you're at it, enjoy every twist and turn and hold your loved ones close. You'll have people in your life that will bring you the wildest times, and the biggest laughs, and some of whom you'll have to let go of. You don't need to do cartwheels anymore for others' validation. You're already worthy. Embrace every opportunity and challenge that comes your way, for they are the building blocks of your future self.

I love you, now love yourself,

Me

DO SOMETHING THAT YOUR FUTURE SELF WILL THANK YOU FOR.
Letter to my future self

Dear Me,

I'm already excited because you're helping so many people, you don't even realize it. Fear is on your shoulder, and the possibility of this disease flaring up. Remember that worry can bring you right back down to where you started. Remember the steps and insights you've gained, and you'll continue to evolve. Take care of your body and don't forget to ask for help. You don't have to suffer alone anymore.

You're a light worker. You're resilient and humble. You don't have to change for anyone else's approval. Use the unique gifts you were born with. Follow your heart and your gut and you'll continue to fulfill your purpose. Remember to be kind to yourself, and never forget the lessons and experiences that have made you who you are today.

These are some of the insights you have learned through experience, and they've served you well:

1. **The ultimate secret to changing your life was realizing your mindset influenced everything. From the moment you wake up until the moment you crawl into bed, everything in between is up to you. This includes your emotions, thoughts, perception, assumptions and whether you respond or react. In every moment, in every day.**

2. Ask yourself WAIT-What Am I Thinking and WAIT-Why Am I Talking? When you reframe your words, you change your thoughts, and it will change your life.

3. Time is priceless and health is precious, so make every moment count. The road you travel will have twists and turns, so take time to enjoy the ride before you run out of gas and your journey ends.

4. You'll never know how strong you are until you're broken; you never know how much you're loved until you lose it. Keep those in your life that give you strength and let go of anything that tears you down.

5. People won't remember what job you had, or what name brand you wore, but they will always remember the way you made them feel.

6. In every single thing you do, you're constantly making a decision that will determine a direction. Your life is a result of each choice.

7. The most valuable things in life are not possessions, but the people we love and the memories we create with others. Remember, you don't know what people are going through behind closed doors.

8. It's not about making the best life; it's making the best out of life every day!

9. The greatest gift you can give someone is your time and attention.

10. The key to happiness is gratitude. Appreciate what you have, and you'll always have enough.

11. If you want to suffer, live in the past. If you want to be stressed, live in the future. The key to happiness is when you let go of both and make the best of the present moment. Ask yourself, "Will this matter in five years?"

12. I would rather be remembered for overcoming my tragedies than being a victim of them. Remember, just because you hear a hoof doesn't mean it's a horse. It could be a zebra.

13. Be open to different modalities of healing, it will offer you a whole new world of options.

14. Sometimes you have to lose HOPE (Heck Over Pleasing Everyone) to find HOPE (Hold On Pain Ends).

15. Make it a priority to strive to be in a feel-good state.

16. Forgiveness isn't about letting go of the past, it's about freeing yourself from the pain it holds over you.

17. Develop a relationship with the God, universe, higher power that you resonate with. Have faith that everything is unfolding for your highest good. Embrace uncertainty.

Skip The Pain, Experience The Pleasure

18. Perfectionism is an illusion that holds us back from reaching our full potential. Dare to take risks and make mistakes to unleash the extraordinary within you. Sometimes the most perfect moments are perfectly unplanned.

19. The power of starting with small steps as it's easy to feel overwhelmed by the magnitude of your dreams. Remember, everything in life started with one single step.

20. Every day we consciously or unconsciously fulfill our purpose by simply being ourselves and sharing our unique gifts with the world to make a difference in the lives of those around us.

21. Remember that it is far more fulfilling to embrace the ability to find peace rather than sprinting to claim the trophy of being right. Some relationships can be destroyed from this simple lesson.

22. It doesn't matter what color you are, what job you have, where you live, or if you have a disability. My wish is that even though there may be a group of people who do wrong and hurtful things, it doesn't mean you paint the entire group with the same brush. We are all humans first.

And don't forget, life is not just about existing. It's about truly living your purpose, finding miracles in every moment, trusting your intuition, letting go of judgment, and creating the best life you can imagine. With excitement in your heart and a burning desire in your soul, there's nothing you can't achieve. So go

Don't Let Others Hold the Pen

out there and make the most of every opportunity, embrace every challenge, and never forget to be open to anything, because anything is possible.

I believe in you.

Love,

Me

Skip The Pain, Experience The Pleasure

> "First, I was dying to finish high school and start college. And then I was dying to finish college and start working. And then I was dying to marry and have children. And then I was dying for my children to grow old enough for school so I could return to work. And then I was dying to retire. And now, I'm dying…and suddenly I realized I forgot to live."
>
> UNKNOWN

Please don't let this happen to you. Appreciate everything around you, the good, especially the good people, and the bad, it doesn't matter. It's what you make of it.

IN THE END, IT'S NOT THE YEARS IN A LIFE; IT'S THE LIFE IN THE YEARS.

TOP 10 THINGS PEOPLE SAID AT THE END OF THEIR LIFE

1. I wish I had dared to live a life true to myself, not the life others expected of me.

When people realize that their life is almost over and look back clearly on it, it's easy to see how many dreams have gone unfulfilled. Most people had not honored even half of their dreams and had to die knowing that it was due to choices they had made, or not made.

2. I wish I hadn't worked so hard.

Not one person said I wish I worked more, had a bigger house, nicer car, or more money in the bank. They worked in jobs they hated and usually worked up to 70 hours per week. Many didn't even use up their vacation time. The most common regret was they missed so much of their children's and partners' lives. They felt they wasted time doing what they felt they needed to, not what they loved.

3. I wish I'd dared to express my feelings and tell others I love them more.

So many people talked about grudges and resentments they had towards others. They could barely remember the details except they spent so much time in hate and anger and less time in love. Love was another biggie. "I love you," is what they would have said more often.

4. I wish I had stayed in touch with my friends.

There were many deep regrets about letting friendships go, especially those they cared for the most. It was easier to say, "We'll get together then," but then never came. Everyone misses their friends when they're dying.

5. I wish that I had let myself be happier.

This was in the top five because so many people felt they had to fit into a cookie-cutter life instead of being authentic. They said they wished they laughed more, did their favorite hobbies, taught, or coached others, or spent their time playing instead of cleaning or being so serious. Many included following their passion.

6. I wish I took better care of my body.

They felt they abused it instead of keeping it strong. So many said their final years were limited by what they could do because they failed to exercise, have a good diet (but still had cake too!), and had other habits that caused more illness. So many people said they wish they got checked out more from a doctor earlier, instead of fluffing their symptoms off.

7. I wish I said "yes" more.

This was close to letting me be happier, but it was distinctly different. It had to do with traveling and exploring, even to other places within their own countries. Saying yes to invitations to join others, saying yes to playing with their kids or going out on more dates (or having date nights with their partners), or stopping by at a friend's or family's when they said to stop by any time. Instead, they said no, mostly out of fear, or feeling it wasn't a big deal. It wasn't until they looked back that they wished they would have said yes and done it!

8. I wish I took more risks.

This was interesting because it ranged from flying an airplane, bungee jumping, or jumping out of an airplane, to risking being rejected for trying something new, like a different career path, getting married, or writing that book, even if no one reads it.

9. I wish I had more gratitude for what I had.

It's easy to be jealous and work hard to keep up with others, but those are things. Instead, many said they took what they had for granted and often overlooked how the simple things were worth a lot. Even if it was waking up the next day.

10. I wish I would have expressed my dying wishes to my family while I could.

They often feel bad knowing that the family is suffering, and the burden they may go through trying to figure out the next moves. Also, knowing the funeral and distribution of items (if any) was a concern.

CONCLUSION

THIS ISN'T A MAGIC BOOK, BUT IT CAN BRING MAGIC INTO YOUR LIFE. YOU CHOOSE.

Take a magic wand, say abracadabra, and poof—you created something. It could have been finishing this book, making something you've been drooling over, or just wasting those three seconds saying abracadabra! One way or another, you spent your time creating or wasting it.

Add some zest to your life! You can be happy and terrified at the same time! Use every emotion, potion, and lotion, heck; throw in some chocolate if that brings you happiness, peace, love, and joy in every area of your life.

Now that you know the blueprint for shifting away from staying stuck in past pain and tragedies to staying in the present and

Skip The Pain, Experience The Pleasure

creating a new script for your future, you can't UN-know it. It's like trying to lick your own elbow, you just can't.

We each have a story, and I hope by sharing some things I've learned as well as some things I've gone through, I can inspire others. Now that you're fully aware of the greatness you have inside you and how much you impact the world just by being in it, you'll feel amazing and can be the best version of yourself.

Where am I now? I'm still learning how to deal with the symptoms of my disease but continue to look for ways to heal. I am completely open to new modalities and excited to watch how healthcare changes and people find ways to cope with whatever life throws at them.

I still have days that I have flare-ups and difficulty walking and talking, but I don't let these episodes ruin my whole life! Sometimes I sit for a few hours, or it might mean I need to rest for a day. No two days are alike. Yesterday I was shopping for a ceiling fan and came home and had to lay down on the hardwood floor as my world was spinning, I was shaking, and my energy was sucked out of me. To the outside world, I looked fine. Remember, you don't always know what someone is going through behind closed doors. Having said that, there are times when I feel fantastic and I'm grateful for those days!

I use my experience, strength and hope to inspire others who may be able to identify with some of the feelings I've had, even if the stories are different. What it all boils down to is that I've learned that I had to cut the crap that was holding me back, so I could live the life I love!

Conclusion

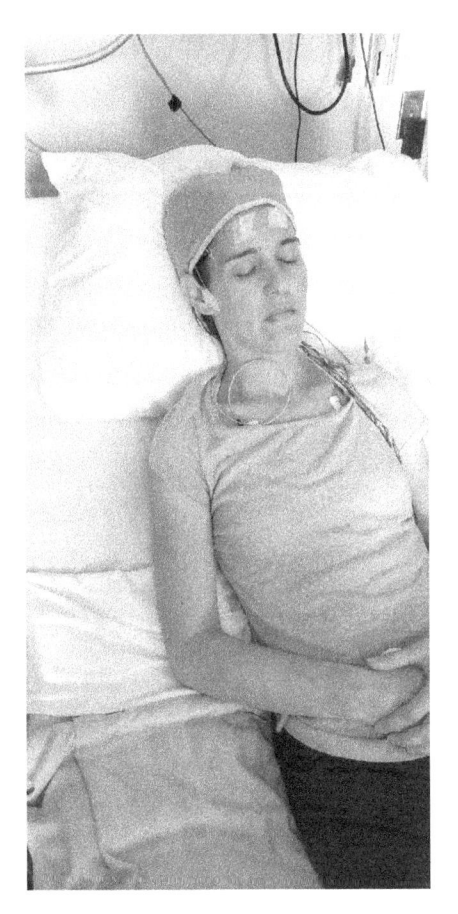

Now it's your decision. Practice using some of these tools to set you up for a better outcome, or not. Oh, and spoiler alert: all will work out in the end!

Only you can choose to *Skip the Pain and Experience the Pleasure!*

Actual pictures of before I started my healing journey.

MORE TESTIMONIALS

Christa not only imparts lessons in coping but also unveils a roadmap to flourish, breaking free from the past with an unstoppable attitude.

Through her anecdotes Christa weaves laughter and invaluable wisdom amidst life's most harrowing trials, and illuminates the way to discover yourself, nurture hope, and embrace the metamorphosis of Skip the Pain, Experience the Pleasure".

Vivienne Mason, Author – Melbourne, Australia.

"What a brilliant read! It shifted my life to gratitude."

Tim Penner, – Ontario, Canada

"A short and easy read that had so much impact! I now have more awareness on my perspective in life."

Richard Henry – Canada

Christa's story about her journey in life is an inspirational tale of pain, hardships, grief, and chronic illness but where there could be depression and resentment, she has substituted joy and acceptance. She has a unique way of finding the bright side when all seems dark and she never plays the victim, although she clearly could have.

Her humour and lightness come through the pages and has you rooting for her every (painful) step of the way. She is a perfect example of how our thoughts become our reality and so she has created a reality that inspires. Her love of life and her family is palpable, her desire to help others through sharing her story, courageous. Her messages of positivity and bravery are what I hope all readers will take away from it, I know I did.

Wendy Boode
Boodeful Inc.
Psycho Spiritual Addiction Recovery Coach
Functional Nutrition Counselor

"This book is a gem. Very profound message wrapped in entertaining wit!"

Satheesh Gopolan, – Ontario, Canada"

More Testimonials

"This book had me in stitches. A short read and full of wisdom."
Booth Stares – Canada

"Amazing lesson on how a change in perspective can open the door to such joy!"
Linda Kim – Canada

"Skip the pain, experience the pleasure" is an evocative and deeply personal journey that tugs at the heartstrings from the very first page. Christa masterfully intertwines the tale of an accident on the first day of spring with a profound exploration of personal trauma, recovery, and self-realization.

The book's opening is undeniably gripping, placing the reader in the middle of a serene winter landscape that swiftly turns treacherous. The ensuing car accident serves as both a literal and metaphorical crossroads in Christa's life. The raw depiction of pain, both physical and emotional, is haunting. The narrative delves deep into the themes of denial, resilience, and the struggle for self-acceptance amidst life's unpredictable trials.

The author's portrayal of addiction and its accompanying denial is both genuine and poignant. The acronymic interpretations of words like "FINE" and "DENIAL" give readers fresh perspectives on familiar feelings, inviting introspection and empathy.

What truly stands out is the book's sincere approach to the healing process. Through memories of youthful adventures and the renewed spark of spontaneity with her husband, Christa's path to recovery is depicted not as a straight road, but a scenic route filled with detours, discoveries, and moments of profound insight.

For anyone who's ever felt trapped by their past, sought validation, or struggled with self-worth, this book is a resounding testament to the power of resilience and the beauty of rediscovery. It's not just a book; it's an experience that leaves a lasting impact. Highly recommended.

Tina Brigley is a leadership coach, TedX Speaker and has been featured in prominent magazines like Forbes, USA Today and Global Woman.

ABOUT THE AUTHOR

Christa was born and raised in Ontario, Canada. Throughout her life, she learned to be resilient. From an unstable childhood and head-on collision, she spiraled down into addiction and became a widow and single parent at the age of 24. Her story was written about in another book to inspire others to find hope through loss, as well as in published poems.

Christa became a Nutrition Manager and worked in a hospital for nine years. Then, with a team, she successfully opened two long-term care homes where she became the director.

Her passion for helping others has come through in her jobs as a Certified Coach Practitioner and Leadership Coach. She specializes as a Mindset Strategist, and Empowerment Coach using her gift of intuition to find clarity and direction in all areas of life.

Skip The Pain, Experience The Pleasure

After already being diagnosed with Lyme disease and fibromyalgia years later, she suffered for three years before she was finally diagnosed with a rare disease called Anti-Gad 65. She went through seizures, paralysis, depression, and loss of eyesight, speech, fine motor skills, muscle pain and so much more. Christa endured intense treatments and went through conventional medicines before entering the world of Energy Work, where she began to recover. She hopes to bring awareness to rare diseases, as they are often overlooked.

She is a Practitioner in Reiki, The Radiance Technique ®, and Access Bars, and holds certificates in Reflexology, and of Natural Medicine.

Christa's passion continues to inspire others through speaking engagements for corporations, retreats, small venues, and non-profit agencies. She also runs workshops that are both engaging and informative.

She is determined to make this world a better place with a goal of planting 100,000 trees around the world. Christa is empowered to inspire others by being the author of *Skip the Pain, Experience the Pleasure; cut the crap that's holding you back so you can live the life you love!*

Christa

Christa is the author of the best-selling book *Skip The Pain, Experience The Pleasure, cut the crap that's holding you back so you can live the life you love.*

From the moment Christa steps on stage, she compels audiences to laugh while they learn. An engaging and down-to-earth speaker, Christa easily connects with audiences of any size and demographic. Through corporate talks, intimate venues, and nonprofit events, she leaves them with empowering tools long after the lights go out.

Christa's life has been filled with challenges, some of which include a head-on collision, losing her spouse at just 24, battling Lyme disease, and uncovering a rare condition called Anti-Gad 65. But she doesn't let these setbacks define her. With a blend of humor and wisdom, she tells her story of bouncing back from rock bottom to reaching soaring heights. Christa focuses on how she became resilient by sharing the lessons she learned along the way, empowering audiences to step up and actively shape their own lives.

Christa's skills include being a Nutrition Manager, Certified Coach Practitioner and Leadership Coach. She specializes as a Mindset Strategist, and Empowerment Coach using her gift of intuition to find clarity and direction in all areas of life. She is a Practitioner in Reiki, The Radiance Technique ®, and Access Bars, and holds certificates in Reflexology, and of Natural Medicine.

Christa aspires to plant 100,000 trees worldwide to better our planet.

Although Christa is able to cater a presentation or keynote to suit any audience, her most powerful talks include:

1. The Pain: Unmasking Identities and Going from Breakdown to Breakthrough.

2. The Promise: Shifting Mindsets and the Way You Talk for Personal Transformation.

3. The Pleasure: Embracing Fear and Crafting an Authentic Life.

To enquire about booking Christa to speak at your next event, please email messagechrista@gmail.com for pricing and availabilities.

NOTES

Skip The Pain, Experience The Pleasure

Notes

Skip The Pain, Experience The Pleasure

Notes

Printed in the USA
CPSIA information can be obtained
at www.ICGtesting.com
JSHW020309091223
53340JS00002B/3

9 781923 123090